HOT LICKS

HOT LICKS

Lesbian Musicians of Note

Edited by
Lee Fleming

gynergy
books

Edited by: Lynn Henry

Cover art by: Janet Riopelle

Cover photographs by: Azúcar y Crema's photo by Linda Sue Scott, hand-coloured by Deborah St. John; k.d. lang's photo by Albert Sanchez; Cris Williamson & Tret Fure's photo by Irene Young; and Toshi Reagon's photo by Gilad Korinsky, hand-coloured by Wayne Crouse.

Printed and bound in Canada by: Best Book Manufacturers

gynergy books acknowledges the generous support of the Canada Council.

Published by:
gynergy books
P.O. Box 2023
Charlottetown, P.E.I.
Canada, C1A 7N7

Canadian Cataloguing in Publication Data
Main entry under title:
Hot licks
    ISBN 0-921881-42-8
1. Lesbian musicians. I. Fleming, Lee, 1957-
ML55.H67 1996   780'.86643   C96-950120-X

Acknowledgements

This book project could not have been completed without the work of Sibyl Frei, managing editor at gynergy books, and Lynn Henry, editor. Thanks for your attention to detail and dedication to excellence. Cudos to Janet Riopelle at gynergy books, for yet another original and pleasing book design.

Many other people helped me in many different ways, among them: Line Chamberline, Zoe Welch, Josée Belleau, Vicki Starr, Rosamund Elwin, Susan Sturman, Larry Wanagas, Alix Dobkin, Dulce Benavides, Nancy Poole, Dr. Ruth Simkin, Cynthia White, Frances Rand from Lesbians on the Loose (Australia), the gals at the Michigan Womyn's Music Festival, *Girlfriend* magazine, *Curve* magazine, Ladyslipper Records and Spinifex.

Thanks to the musicians who were willing to be involved in this project, despite their very demanding schedules.

And a nod of respect to the managers of the participating musicians — they are the unsung support person(s) who work tirelessly behind the scenes for their artists. Finally, I'd like to thank my lover, Heidi Rankin, for ongoing love and support.

Table of Contents

Dear Reader

Y ou are holding in your hands the first-ever anthology entirely devoted to lesbian musicians. In its pages, you'll find twenty-three profiles of out and proud dyke performers, who clearly demonstrate that they can not only deliver great music to their listening fans but also tell engaging stories to their reading public. Here are hot pics, fan info, lyrics and stories from musicians in Canada, the United States, Australia, New Zealand, Scotland and Ireland. Their musical styles include: folk; blues; salsa; technopop/fusion; country and western; rock 'n' roll and punk/riot grrl music. What do these performers have in common? They have all worked hard, followed their dreams and publicly acknowledged their sexual orientation.

I was inspired to produce *Hot Licks* for two reasons. First, I am a musician myself and, at this relatively late stage in life (I will be thirty-nine as this book goes into print), I have thrown myself off the cliff of security to pursue my long-held musical dream — to become a full-time professional musician. Naturally, I wanted to find out more about the experiences of established, dedicated musicians who are lesbians (and, equally important to me, lesbians who are musicians). Second, like many musicians, I have "other irons in the fire" and, as I pursue my musical goals, I

continue to edit books. I decided to combine my two passions in an editing project that would allow readers to enjoy the thematic connections that an anthology so uniquely and wonderfully provides. Fortunately, my publisher, gynergy books, quickly embraced the idea for *Hot Licks* and the work began.

Certain key editorial questions guided the development of this book: What does it mean at the end of this century to be a lesbian (or dyke, or queer) musician? What comes first, the music or the lesbian identity? How do the two co-exist? How has the 1970s phenomenon of "women's music" changed the lives of those who were involved in it, and informed the work of the younger generation of musicians? I wanted to engage each contributor in the act of sitting down and writing about these questions in a thoughtful manner. For that reason, the pieces in this book are different from magazine articles that I have read, where interviews are directed by the journalist. On the contrary, in this book the "A Capella" stories were composed by the performers themselves. Each of them sat down with pen or word processor or talked with me and candidly shared their lives. The result is the best I could have hoped for: a timely statement that will endure in collectors' hands for years to come.

Hot Licks documents a piece of our history, our culture, our story. Other books will, and must, follow — this anthology is by no means comprehensive, and it includes a large number of musicians who might be classified under the catch-all "folk" label. Nonetheless, I find myself amazed at its diversity. It contains the voices of those who've been around from the beginning of "women's music": lesbians like Alix Dobkin, who, along with Kay Gardner, kicked it all off in 1973 with *Lavender Jane Loves Women*; Cris Williamson, whose 1974 recording, *The Changer and the Changed*, is arguably the single most significant vinyl recording ever made by any lesbian; and Cris's partner, Tret Fure — herself well known and respected in the "women's music" scene — who, with Cris, stays true to herself. Ferron, Judy Small, Heather Bishop and Faith Nolan, who have all been recording since the early 1980s, continue to record new, superb songs. All of them act as our wise women, our storytellers, our web weavers.

There are those who have been around equally as long — or longer — but who have only recently come out or been "outed." Each was quickly signed to a major record label relatively early in her career. These include the one and only k.d. lang; Janis Ian, who has forty distinguished years in the business; and Geneviève Paris, much appreciated in Quebec as a superb guitarist, songwriter and performer. In the early and mid-1980s, many out lesbian artists established themselves with a wider public, and they too are represented here: lesbians like Phranc, the Topp Twins, Jennifer Berezan, and Toshi Reagon. Hot on their heels came "in-your-face," wild, electric music, as bands like Girls in the Nose, Tribe 8, Random Order and Well Oiled Sisters began to emerge in the late 1980s and early 1990s. Today, there is a diverse profusion of musicians — so many that one can hardly keep up. Among the newer artists included here are Azúcar y Crema, Melissa Ferrick, Nedra Johnson, Connie Lofton, Wyrd Sisters and Zrazy, all of whom began recording in the 1990s.

In the end, the beauty of this book is the opportunity it provides for the reader to see many parts of a constantly evolving whole — the similarities and vast differences; the musical evolution that occurs with time and experience; and the glimmerings of what music is still to be created. Even if we're not "into" the music that some of these contributors play, we cannot help but be moved and inspired by their courage. Each one has worked hard and long to honour her calling. It is not surprising, therefore, that there is a unifying theme and philosophy in this book — one that clearly puts integrity and honesty before material gain and "stardom." These artists encourage all of us, seasoned professionals and "wannabe" amateurs alike, to practise hard, have fun and respect ourselves and others.

My inspiration for *Hot Licks* was a desire to document — to take a literary "sound bite" of — the richly diverse and ever-expanding world of dyke music. I hope you find inspiration from the musicians who make up *Hot Licks*.

Lee Fleming
July 1996

LINDA SUE SCOTT

Azúcar y Crema

Azúcar y Crema (Spanish for "sugar and cream") is a seven-piece, multicultural ensemble of *Salseras* from the San Francisco Bay area. Each members of Azúcar y Crema is a multi-talented musician, artist and activist in her own right. Formed in January 1991, this stimulating group of women combines Afro/Cuban rhythms, harmonic voices and energetic, intricate horn phrasing — a powerful and irresistible Latin extravaganza! ◄

Clockwise from top left: Robin, María, Suki, Mary, Tami, Rémy, Cathi

making music

María Cora
Lead vocals, percussion

Tami Ellis
Trumpet, back-up vocals

Mary Gemini
Keyboards, back-up vocals

Cathi Ramos
Timbales, small percussion, bongos, campana

Rémy Rodriguez
Band leader, vocals, piano, bass

Robin Nziazah Smith
Saxophone, flute, hand percussion, back-up vocals

Suki (aka Sue Kaye)
Congas, percussion, back-up vocals

A Capella (Rémy Rodriguez)

Sugar, Cream and the Strength of Family

Throughout my life, music has been a daily ritual. As a young musician, I had to practise every day, and music was a constant in our household. My mother had a wonderful voice. She sang from the moment she woke up to the time she went to bed. We just didn't let a day go by without salsa, classical, jazz and contemporary music being played in the house. My mom's positive light and energy still flourish inside of me, reminding me to keep on going forward and creating. *My abuelita* Elia's determination, strong will and indomitable spirit have also stayed with me. My ancestors have given me strength and they guide me in the path that I take: *Gracias a mis santos* for shadowing me throughout my life.

My musical roots stem from my classical training, which began when I was five. I studied piano privately for twelve years and performed in classical music recitals from the age of seven. As a young musician I was inspired by the great classical composers — Beethoven, Brahms, Bach, Chopin, Mozart, Liszt. In my teenage years I began composing non-classical pieces and playing jazz keyboard, and when I attended college I played and studied jazz, but it wasn't until 1976, when I relocated to San Francisco from DC, that I began performing in salsa groups. Some of my favourite jazz and Latin composers are Chick

▶ **OPENING NOTES**
[Rémy Rodriguez]

Date of birth
October 1, 1956

Place of birth
Washington, DC, USA

Astrological sign
Libra

Heritage
Cubana, Sicilian

Siblings
None

Languages
English, Spanish

Current residence
Washington, DC, USA

▶ ▶ ▶

Corea, Herbie Hancock, Papo Luca, Oscar Hernández, Alfredo Valdez and Janis Ian, to mention a few. I was and am greatly inspired by Cuban composers — my influences are very Cuban, and this is evident in my compositions. My preference now is to listen to salsa.

Today, I create and develop my music through hard work and endurance. Azúcar y Crema (Sugar and Cream) is the first band that I have led, directed and written for with vigour and drive. The mere fact that the same seven women have been together for five years is a statement in itself. That we've stayed together can be attributed in part to the long and arduous process of choosing the members for the band. Our great diversity of heritage, musical ability and musical background enables Azúcar y Crema to be the fabulous group that it is. Several of us had performed together in different groups at various times; however, coming together as Azúcar y Crema deepened the bonds between us. *Somos familia* (We are family). We love one another as family, with all the ups, downs and in-betweens that go along with that. One of the rules in the band

is that we cannot be lovers with each other. All the members of the band are thankful and appreciative of the flexibility and support shown by the women who do choose to share their lives with us. Relationships, like people, have to experience

· · · · · · · · · · · ·

"My hope is ... to be an inspiration to others through my music."

· · · · · · · · · · · ·

change, and this is especially true in relationships with musicians. It takes a strong person to be with a musician.

I myself am strong in my desire to love women, and to write about and for them. As an out lesbian band in a musical genre

with few women musicians and almost no out lesbians, we carry a strong message to our community. An Azúcar y Crema audience is teeming with diversity: Straight men and women dance alongside lesbians; Latinos, Anglos and African-Americans share the dance floor. The world would be a better place if there was the kind of acceptance of diversity that we exemplify in our music and performances. In the meantime, I'll continue to speak the truth from my experiences, and hopefully influence those in my life, and those who pass through my life, with my music and lyrics.

Azúcar y Crema gives me the opportunity to realize my writing potential and allows my creations to be heard. The wonderful thing about composing for this particular group of women is that their musical expertise — and my knowledge of their abilities and potential — not only

· ·

Discography

- **To Olidia, with Love**/self-produced, 1993

· ·

allows me to express myself, but allows the members of the band to shine. Maria Cora, our lead singer, has been very inspirational to me as a lyricist. One of her strengths is her ability to improvise lyrics, which is an essential part of being a *sonera* (female salsa singer). She sings about the potential for positive change, while educating us about past oppressions. When all our strengths as musicians come together, it is a magical occurrence. Some of our most memorable performances have been at the Michigan Womyn's Music Festival. Playing for all those women — what a charge! How often do musicians get to play in lace bras and leather pants or fishnet stockings and a camisole? We've played all over the United States for various gay and lesbian events: Gay Pride celebrations, LAVA awards, LLEGO conferences and a variety of other engagements.

Sometimes I think that it's amazing that Azúcar y Crema is still together, given all of life's changes and the difficult challenges we have faced individually this year. This last year was especially hard on me because of the loss of my mother almost one year ago, on June 21,

1995. I had to uproot my life in the Bay Area and go to the East Coast to deal with my mother's legal affairs. I have also struggled with choices I have made in my relationships with women, and I have also come to understand that change

- - - - - - - - - - - - -

"This world needs more acceptance of diversity."

- - - - - - - - - - - - -

is the only constant in life. The trick is to learn how to move easily through the changes.

Through everything, my mother's strength and positive outlook on life have remained with me and made me determined to keep Azúcar y Crema alive. I believe that communication is the essence of understanding one another, and music is the one language that has no barriers: The spectrum of emotions can be expressed through music. Having the ability to play and create compositions allows

me to express myself; it's a high that no drug can reproduce. I've been a rebel from day one, and I will continue to be a devoted musician and a good lover. It is a gift for me to be a musician — one of cellular familiarity — and something I'll do until the day I die. My hope is to make a difference in the world and to be an inspiration to others through my music. This world needs more acceptance of diversity, and more powerful women taking charge.

My motto is: *Ache*. Power to women. ◄

Fan Fare

Agent
326 Sheridan St. N.W., Washington, DC, USA, 20011-133; (202) 291-9412 *and* 1811 W. Silverlake Dr., Los Angeles, CA, USA, 90026; (213) 660-5619

Orders
Ladyslipper Music, P.O. Box 3124, Durham, NC, USA, 27715-3124; 1-800-634-6044

E-mail
ladyslip@nando.net

14

Hot Pick

Sabrina

Rémy Rodriguez

Voy a cantar una melodia
para recordar a mis memórias
y quiero saber en que tu piensas
porque yo pensao de ti

Coro:
Dime si tu quieres tirar una
huerta otra vez Mamita
Dime si tu quieres tirar una huerta
Oye Sabrina
Dime que si — Mamita
Dime que si — Sabrina
Si tu quieres, si tu quieres
Si tu quieres bailar

Pues vamos a ver
Si la melodia
Se va a caer arriba de ti
pero que vacilon — bailando contigo
Sabrina, si tu quieres bailar

[Coro]

Escuchalo bien esta canción
que yo canto
para saber si tu quieres;
si tu quieres bailar
Con Azúcar y Crema
oyelo; si; te va a gustar

Con Mary, Suki, Tami, Robin,
Cathi, Rémy y yo

[Coro]

© Rémy Rodriguez, 1993

Sabrina

[English translation by Rémy Rodriguez]

I'm going to sing a melody
to bring back the memories
and I want to know
what you're thinking
because I'm thinking of you

Now, listen up good
to what I'm singing
because I want to know
I want to know; if you want
to dance
with Azúcar y Crema
yes, you're going to enjoy this

Chorus:
Tell me, do you want to take a
spin another time with me, Mami
Tell me do you want to take a spin
oh, Sabrina
Tell me yes, Mami
Tell me yes, Sabrina
if you want; if you want
if you want to dance

With Mary, Suki, Tami, Robin
Cathi, Rémy y yo

[Chorus]

© Rémy Rodriguez, 1993

Well, let's see
if the melody
will put you under my spell
And what a great time I'll
have, dancing with you, Sabrina
tell me, if you want to dance

[Chorus]

Jennifer Berezan

From her prairie roots in Alberta, Canada, to her present-day urban life in Oakland, California, Jennifer Berezan has acquired a broad base of experiences to draw upon in her music. She has earned international praise for her original contribution to progressive music, and the respect for life and love of women that is an integral part of her songs.

Jennifer Berezan released her first album, *In the Eye of the Storm*, in 1989 on her own label. The album combined original material with cover songs and demonstrated Berezan's interest in spirituality and politics. Berezan's second album, *Borderlines*, was produced by Mike Marshall, a Windham Hill recording artist. Says Berezan, "I knew more of what I wanted with this album.

There's a song about homelessness called 'Shadows on the Street.' Another song is a reaction to the Gulf War, and a piece called 'One and One Makes Three' takes a look at fundamentalism of various stripes." *Borderlines* was nominated for a 1992 NAIRD (National Association of Independent Record Distributors) award in the adult/contemporary category.

In her recent work, Jennifer Berezan prefers interacting with audiences. For the past several years, she has been working with author Vicki Noble on a multimedia piece involving a slide show and a healing circle that includes drumming and chanting. "A concert is an interesting dynamic," she says. "You create this circle with the audience and for two hours you are immersed in this womb-like entity. It's interactive because we give a lot to each other. I leave feeling very full and that's a real gift." ◄

► OPENING NOTES

Date of birth
January 19, 1961

Place of birth
Edmonton, AB, Canada

Astrological sign
Capricorn

Heritage
Polish, Ukrainian

Siblings
Three brothers

Language
English

Current residence
Oakland, CA, USA

Instruments
Guitar, vocals

► ► ►

Sound and Spirit

My involvement with music began in the late 1960s and early 1970s, when the A.M. airwaves were carrying great songs by singer-songwriters as well as bands. I listened to everyone from the Beatles to Joni Mitchell, Neil Young, Carole King, Gordon Lightfoot and Cat Stevens. I think that, subliminally, these songs I heard over the radio were my earliest influences, along with the traditional folk tunes that I played out of music books as a child. I began playing the guitar when I was six years old, after a travelling music saleswoman came to our house. She gave me a "musical aptitude test" and told my parents I had great potential. I'm sure she told that to all the moms and dads, but it was all that was needed to get me

taking guitar lessons and singing. In high school, I discovered the folk revival of the 1960s and went crazy over Bob Dylan, Joan Baez and Woody Guthrie — their music politicized me. I was stunned when I discovered this music. I was just becoming socially aware and politically conscious. I went back and rediscovered the whole American 1960s experience through the

music. I began writing songs when I was in that adolescent-angst period. I needed an outlet for a lot of emotional stuff that was going on in my life.

I had a brief punk phase in the late 1970s, and later I discovered Bruce Cockburn, who was a huge influence. Then, when I became a feminist, the whole world of women's music was

Discography

- **In the Eye of the Storm**/Edge of Wonder Records, 1989
- **Borderlines**/Flying Fish Records, 1992
- **Voices on the Wind**/Edge of Wonder Records, 1993
- **She Carries Me** (with Olympia Dukakis, Chris Webster and Darol Anger)/Edge of Wonder Records, 1995
- **The Turning of the Wheel**/1997 release

Jennifer **Berezan**

opened up to me. It was amazing to find singers like Ferron, Holly Near and Meg Christian. Now I am inspired by world music and anything with a lot of soul and power to heal. And I still love the energy of rock 'n' roll.

My first performances were in school coffee houses and church choirs. Then, when I was backpacking through Europe a few years later, I played on the streets. This was great because it was a performance setting, but you could pack up and leave at any moment. Since then I've performed at many folk festivals, women's festivals, clubs and colleges throughout North America and Europe.

My interests have always included both music and spirituality. In my early twenties, I was studying at the University of Alberta and became very interested in the treatment of women by the major religions. By my final year at the university, it had become my complete obsession. I took a lot of women's studies classes and found that religion has played an incredible role in keeping women oppressed throughout history. Ten years ago, I moved to Oakland, California, to pursue

a master's degree at the Institute in Creation Spirituality at Holy Names College. It was run by a renegade Catholic priest whose program involved not only academic study, but experiential, hands-on artistic and spiritual practices. There was a focus on political awareness as well. I was very drawn

. . . .

"I began playing the guitar ... after a travelling music saleswoman came to our house."

. . . .

to that, and it's what initially brought me to California. I didn't hook up with the Bay Area music scene until my second year here. My first gig was a double bill with fellow Canadian Lucie Blue Tremblay at the Valencia Rose in San Francisco. After that, I played at local clubs and restaurants and built up a following.

Increasingly, I am finding ways to bring these interests together in my work. Recently I recorded and produced a project entitled *She Carries Me* with my friend Chris Webster, who also contributed stunning vocals. The recording is a meditation on the Goddess in her many forms, and includes layers of instrumentation and vocals as well as a beautiful spoken part by the actor Olympia Dukakis. Olympia recites "The Charge of the Goddess" on top of tracks of instrumentation and chanting. It also features a group of women chanting a vesper-like chorus that is a feminist reworking of the "Hail Mary." Because this music is hard to present live, I organized one big event in which more than fifty singers and dancers came together to perform the piece as a community ritual and benefit for the Women's Forest Sanctuary. That has definitely been one of the performing highlights of my life.

In my spare time, I am really into gardening; it saved me one year during a very difficult emotional time and now I am madly obsessed with flowers. I also lead a music and healing workshop for women entitled

J e n n i f e r   **B e r e z a n**

"The Ecstasy of Sound" and I do a lot of research into ancient Goddess-centred civilizations. In fact, I am somewhat of an amateur archaeologist and have led tours for women to sacred Goddess sights in places like Malta, Ireland and Greece. Singing in a circle of women in 7,000-year-old Goddess temples has been a remarkable and life-changing experience.

For me, music is a form of spiritual practice and a way to express political and personal feelings. I believe that people write from their own experience, and politics and spiritually have always been much more than academic study for me. At times, I have been on a completely obsessive quest to try to figure out what happened on this planet. I've come to believe that war and injustice are not "natural" to the human condition but were outgrowths of patriarchal systems that took

hold only about 6,000 years ago.

I think the urge to create comes from all the feelings I have inside me, demanding to be given a voice. When I speak what I feel is true for me, I feel aligned and integrated. And I hope my music is helpful to others and not just cathartic for me. I want to give something back and be useful. I love the collaborative part of music — collaborating with other musicians on stage or in the studio is magical. I like having salons at my house, where women come together and share their creative projects and ideas. It's this kind of feeling that I also wish to create on stage — a sense of the creative community we lost a long time ago. I play music for the joy of it, for the power it has to heal and create states of ecstasy, and for the sense of community it brings. ◄

21

"The urge to create comes from all the feelings I have inside me."

Fan Fare

Promotion/booking agent
1460 Cornell Ave.,
Berkeley, CA, USA, 94702;
(510) 524-4183

Jennifer **Berezan**

Hot Pick

She Carries Me

Lyrics: Jennifer Berezan
Music: Jennifer Berezan and Chris Webster

She is a boat she is a light
High on a hill in dark of night
She is a wave she is the deep
She is the dark where angels sleep
Where all is still and peace abides
She carries me to the other side

Chorus:
She carries me, she carries me
She carries me to the other side

And though I walk through valleys deep
And shadows chase me in my sleep
On rocky cliffs I stand alone
I have no name, I have no home
With broken wings I reach to fly
She carries me to the other side

[Chorus]

A thousand arms, a thousand eyes
A thousand ears to hear my cries
She is the gate, she is the door
She leads me through and back once more
When day has dawned and death is nigh
She'll carry me to the other side

[Chorus]

She is the first, she is the last
She is the future and the past
Mother of all, of earth and sky
She carries me to the other side

[Chorus]

Heather Bishop

▶ OPENING NOTES

Date of birth
April 25, 1949

Place of birth
Regina, SK, Canada

Astrological sign
Taurus

Heritage
Celtic — Scottish, English, Irish

Siblings
Two brothers

Languages
English, a little French

Current residence
Manitoba, Canada

Instruments
Vocals, acoustic guitar, piano

Heather Bishop is a Canadian musician who writes and sings provocative songs that confront racist and sexist oppression. Her songs are poetic statements filled with insight, humour and passion. Since she began performing in the 1970s, Heather has been an outspoken voice in folk and women's music. And what a voice! She can lay 'em back or belt 'em out with equal ease. One critic has remarked that "nothing compares to the depth, sensuality, and passion of Heather Bishop's vocals. She can sing with a cutting edge, a blues growl or echoing resonance." The *Milwaukee Sentinel* described her as "a true musical artist who can transcend categories and sneak sound past one's psychological barriers." And Kate Clinton states that "Heather is a feast for the ears as well as the soul." ◀

Healing and Resonance

Because I grew up on the prairies, my musical roots are country and old-time. At thirteen, I discovered Nina Simone and I spent the next ten years listening to female blues singers — Ma Rainey, Bessie Smith, Billie Holiday, Nina Simone — all black, of course. I also listened to Buffy Sainte-Marie. In general, my biggest influences were women of colour and my mother's grandmother. Today, I mostly listen to the music of my contemporaries — Connie Kaldor, Ferron, Rhiannon — and I'm still influenced by Buffy Sainte-Marie.

My musical training began when I was five, with piano lessons. Eventually, I finished my Grade Nine Royal Conservatory exam. At fifteen, I began playing guitar and took lessons off and on. Much later — when I was twenty-eight — I also took *bel canto* vocal training for five or six years. My first performance took place at a coffee house when I was still in high school, and I've been performing professionally since 1973. I've been a solo performer for twenty years, since 1976.

I've played at just about every lesbian music festival there ever was, and I've always felt I had an identity as a lesbian musician — always. I came out in 1972 and from day one it has been hard to get the press to look at my music — they've

Discography

- **Grandmother's Song**/Mother of Pearl Records, 1979
- **Celebration**/Mother of Pearl Records, 1980
- **Bellybutton**/Mother of Pearl Records, 1982
- **I Love Women**/Mother of Pearl Records, 1982
- **Purple People Eater**/Mother of Pearl Records, 1985
- **A Taste of the Blues**/Mother of Pearl Records, 1986
- **Walk That Edge**/Mother of Pearl Records, 1988
- **A Duck in New York City**/Mother of Pearl Records, 1989
- **Old New Borrowed Blue**/Mother of Pearl Records, 1992
- **Daydream Me Home**/Mother of Pearl Records, 1994

Heather **Bishop**

> ## "The press [has] been too busy honing in on the fact that I'm out …"

been too busy honing in on the fact that I'm out and always have been.

There have been so many memorable performances over the years: playing with Connie Kaldor and Ferron at the Edmonton Folk Festival, the first time a Canadian festival hired all three of us; sharing a stage at the Winnipeg Folk Festival with Meg Christian, Holly Near, Connie Kaldor and Sweet Honey in the Rock; playing with some of Canada's symphony orchestras; some late-night main-stage moments at the Michigan Festival; the Vancouver Folk Festival; singing with seventy-three men from the Vancouver Men's Chorus; or today's performance in a gym, singing to 150 kids.

These days, I'm on tour and will be doing seventy concerts in three months. I just returned from a month of performances in Australia and have also just finished writing a new kids' album. My next project is to take a year off and write a new adult album. In my spare time I'm a carpenter — I build things, like houses.

I play music because it is the gift I've been given — I am a healer with music, and I could not turn my back on that. My journey is to honour the gift.

> ## "I play music because it is the gift I've been given."

To aspiring lesbian musicians I offer these words: spirit, truth, laughter, pain, power, self-respect, courage — and an opening to great mystery. Truth rings out. When one woman speaks her truth, it resonates in all of us. ◄

Fan Fare

Management
Joan Miller, 1210B Allston Way, Berkeley, CA, USA, 94702; (510) 540-5286

E-mail
HBishopJM@aol.com

Heather **Bishop**

Hot Pick

If You Leave Me Darlin'
Heather Bishop and Joan Miller

You know how hard I try to be who you want me to
be
But I hear you darlin' — sayin' you wanna be free
You feel like a new woman, but honey can't you see
If I weren't busy being you, it'd be a big waste of
me.

Chorus:
If only I could read your mind
I'd know how I feel
If only I could find my boundaries
I'd know what is real
You see I don't know who I am when I'm not with
you
So if you leave me darlin', can I come too?

I have to admit, I think I might be confused
You see I can't always tell any more who's me and
who's you
But I give myself permission to do the best I can do
'Cause when it's all said and done, does it really
matter who's who?

[Chorus]

I can tell that you've been sayin' yes, but you're
feelin' no
You have to honour your potential now and start
lettin' go
I accept and I acknowledge this and I choose to
grow
I could give up my need to suffer but I'd miss it so.

[Chorus with]
If you leave me darlin', I'm comin' too
You can't leave me darlin', cause I'm leavin' you.

© Heather Bishop/SOCAN, 1992

Heather **Bishop**

Alix Dobkin

A poet of life, love, pain and all the human emotions, Alix Dobkin composes thought-provoking songs that span all ages. She was one of the first singer-songwriters anywhere to unabashedly depict the experiences of women loving women. "She is renowned for music with a biting sense of humor, inventive harmonics and melodies, and uncompromising lesbian and feminist lyrics … an imaginative musician whose candid commentaries on women's concerns over the past twenty years have encouraged others to 'speak out'": *New Age Journal*. As *Off Our Backs* once wrote: "Alix is a kick … women love Alix … give me Alix any day!" ◄

► OPENING NOTES

Date of birth
August 16, 1940

Place of birth
New York City, NY, USA

Astrological sign
Leo

Heritage
Jewish

Siblings
One brother, one sister

Languages
English, some Spanish

Current residence
Oakland, CA, USA

Instruments
Vocals, acoustic guitar, yodelling

► ► ►

Lavender Jane Loves Music

I was born on August 16, 1940, while the sun was in Leo with Mars, Mercury and Pluto present, Capricorn ascending, the moon in Aquarius, Saturn and Jupiter conjoining in Taurus, and Venus in Cancer — which means that each element was represented at the time of my birth!

My heritage is that of the New York Radical Jew — to be precise, I was a "red-diaper baby." My parents were a tremendous influence on me. They listened to all kinds of music, had art on the walls and filled many shelves with books and journals. We had constant discussions about everything and did not stand on ceremony or try to make superficial impressions on for anyone. My family was involved with politics, and we children were introduced to cultures around the world and taught to be anti-racist and passionate about social justice. It was important not to hurt people's feelings, to be honest, to laugh and, above all, not be a "phony." We were taught not to waste, to respect working people, world cultures, high standards and down-to-earth values. We moved many times, but I always felt secure at home and sure of my parents' love and acceptance, as well as their high expectations. My mother instituted "family meetings," where we were encouraged to

· · · · · · · · · · · · · · · · · · · ·

Discography

- **Lavender Jane Loves Women**/Women's Wax Works, 1973
- **Living with Lesbians**/Women's Wax Works, 1976
- **XXAlix**/Women's Wax Works, 1980
- **These Women: Never Been Better**/Women's Wax Works, 1986
- **Yahoo Australia**/Women's Wax Works, 1990
- **Love & Politics**/Women's Wax Works, 1992

· · · · · · · · · · · · · · · · · · · ·

Alix **Dobkin**

talk openly about anything that was bothering us. It was not a perfect family, but it was warm and accepting, and my friends were always made to feel comfortable.

My early musical environment was a rich mix that included everything from the Red Army Chorus and songs of the Spanish Civil War to classical music (Bach in particular) to Dixieland (Louis Armstrong in particular). There was always a variety of folk music, specifically Yiddish songs of resistance, Woody Guthrie, Leadbelly, Josh White, Paul Robeson, the union-organizing and "protest" songs of Pete Seeger, the Almanac Singers and the Weavers. I was greatly influenced by Broadway show tunes from *Oklahoma*, *South Pacific*, *The King and I*, *Guys and Dolls* and *Finian's Rainbow*, as well as the musical movies of the 1940s and 1950s. I especially loved the singing of Jane Powell; she was my idol for many years. Later there were Dave Brubeck, Tom Lehrer, Ethel Raim, Peggy Seeger, the Bulgarian Women's Chorus (under the direction of Phillip Koutev), Bob Dylan, Fred Neil, Carolyn Hester, Anita O'Day, Jo Mapes, Aretha Franklin,

> "Nine hundred women from all over Europe were jammed into a dark, smoky hall."

Carmen MacRae and Nina Simone. These days, I listen to k.d. lang, Phranc, Mary Chapin Carpenter, K.T. Oslin, Laura Love, Bonnie Raitt, Varttina, Girls in the Nose, the Maul Girls, the Bulgarian Women's Chorus, Vicki Randle and many, many others.

My mother was a pianist and accomplished musician in her

> "My musical identity has more to do with lesbian politics than with music."

own right. She encouraged me to study piano at the age of eight, and I did for three years, but then I found it too boring and I quit. When I was sixteen, my friend Eliot began taking guitar lessons and passed the lessons on to me; that's how I started playing guitar, and that's when I first performed for pay (with Eliot). My training consisted of watching and stealing from other players and swapping techniques with friends. I still can't read music.

I think my musical "identity" — which is, of course, folk — has more to do with lesbian politics than with music. I came out as a lesbian on Valentine's Day in 1972. Since then, I have performed at practically every lesbian music festival there is. One memorable performance was at a women's festival in Amsterdam in the autumn of 1979. Nine hundred women from all over Europe were jammed into a dark, smoky hall, and when I began to sing "The Woman in Your Life Is You," the whole room joined in. It gave me goose bumps and a terrific light-headedness, and after the show I went straight to the bathroom backstage and threw up from the excitement.

Alix **Dobkin**

> ### "Don't waste my time with something I've already heard!"

Another highlight was playing on the Michigan Festival day stage with the Party Line Dance Band in the early 1980s. (For many years, I played bass and sang lead vocals in the band, alongside musicians Debbie Fier and River Lightwomoon.) I remember hundreds of women kicking up a dust storm. I also remember doing Balkan yells and dissonances with festival audiences.

Recently, I have been developing a workshop called "Vocal Work-out" to uncover and strengthen the muscles of the natural voice, which most of us have neglected since childhood. I have also recently run sound for Iabas, a fantastic ten-woman Brazilian musical group based in Woodstock, NY. In California, where I live, I host a monthly community open mic. In my spare time, I like to read, joke around and analyze stuff with my friends. I live with my partner, Sherry, and her son, Ryan, who are very special to me. Tops on the "special" list are my amazing daughter, Adrian, and her partner, Chris; my brother, Carl, my sister-in-law, Pat, and their daughters, Allison and Loren; my friends River, Susan, Boo and Retts; my dear friend Suzanne, who is much too far away in Australia; and my sister, Julie, and her partner, Debbie.

Why do I play music? To give people another perspective, to help them think, and because I love the attention. I would not be able to live without music. It can go where no other art can, and it has a richer, deeper influence than anything else I can think of. My advice to lesbian musicians — and all artists — is: Don't waste my time with something I've already heard! Be your unique, original self in your own words, in your own voice, in your own style. ◄

Fan Fare

Bookings
Alix Dobkin,
4314 Shafter Ave.,
Oakland, CA, USA, 94609;
(510) 595-7223

Alix **Dobkin**

Hot Pick

Lesbian Code

Alix Dobkin

She's a BD (baby Dyke)
She's a PD (possible, probable)
She's a DD (she's a definite Dyke)
She's a POU (positively one of us)
She's got hi-LP (good [lesbian] potential)
Suffering from PLT (pre-lesbian tension)
She's a wannabe, a DOT
Maybe not a Dyke of Today, but she could be a
    Dyke of Tomorrow
Then she'll be a DIT (Dyke in training)
Or a FDA (future Dyke of America)
She'll be a Betty, a Friend of Dorothy
She'll be Our Kind, that's OK …

Is she Lithuanian? (I don't know)
Is she Lebanese? Well, she's gifted!
She's Lebesian, Lesbonic and I happen to know
She's a vagitarian
She's a member of the club
She's a member of the team, of the family
She's a member of the lodge, of the church, the
    committee
And she sings in the choir
Is she a lima bean? (from Kentucky)
Is she a green new bean, or is she refried?
Is she a canned bean in the closet?
Or is she now with a man? Then she's a hasbean

   Chorus:
   She's a Fresbian in Fresno
   In Lansing: 48912
   She lives in Dyke Heights
   She's an Arkansas Earth Dyke
   motor city Dykette
   She goes to The Pagoda with the Chinese. You bet!
   She colors outside the lines in Charlotte

Is she an Aussie Dyke? Check it out, waddyareckon?
She's a likely one. Spot-o. Gottabe!
She looks a bit sus. She must be of the faith
I'll but her on layby
She's a leesbian from New Zealand
She's campas, a kiwi fruit from Aotearou
You can spot the camp girl, spot the bus driver
She's on the bike. Camp as a row of tents
She's a "how's-your-mother?" over in Dublin
She's a "whatever-you're-having" in Belfast. In Cork
She's a quare girl, a lash, got a glad eye
She's got a kick in her. Drinks Tipperary water

She's the Church of England. She's ginger
She's got Dutch boy fingers
She's a MOT: A member of the tribe
She's a gold star, got her ID card
She shops at Tescoes
A Sister of the inclination
She's elite in Scotland. Auch, eye. Zap!
She's all right. That's 100 points!
Is she a carpenter from Bristol?
Is she a bus driver from Nottingham?
Is she a motor Dyke? Is she a badgy Dyke?
Does she live in the Dykery? Ah, then …

   [Chorus]

© Alix Dobkin, 1990

A l i x   **D o b k i n**

Melissa Ferrick

Twenty-six-year-old Melissa Ferrick may be "the other Melissa" among lesbian musicians right now — but she probably won't be for long. Ferrick got her start in 1990 in Boston, when Morrissey's opening act had to leave for L.A. and, in a panic, the promoter called Ferrick and she became the replacement act. "I remember meeting Morrissey, then I remember walking on stage, then I remember the end of it," recounts Ferrick. Fortunately, the press at the concert didn't forget her performance — Ferrick was hired for the rest of the tour. Soon afterwards, she signed with Atlantic Records and, in 1993, she released her debut album, *Massive Blur*, which won critical acclaim for its accomplished melodies and emotional depth. In her most recent release, *Willing to Wait*, Ferrick demonstrates the maturing of her talent as she sets her lyrics in a spare, acoustic setting, addresses her feelings with wisdom and insight — and invites listeners to look more deeply into her heart. ◄

► OPENING NOTES

Date of birth
September 21, 1970

Place of birth
Haverhill, MA, USA

Astrological sign
Virgo

Heritage
Irish, English, French

Siblings
One sister

Languages
English, a little Spanish

Current residence
West Hollywood, CA, USA

Instruments
Vocals, guitar, bass, trumpet

► ► ►

No Need to Wait

I started playing the violin at age five. I told my parents that I had "wanted to play the violin since before I was born," and they figured that it would be a good idea to get me one. I started playing the trumpet in elementary school, then picked up bass and guitar in high school. I've played the violin for a total of twelve years and I still play the trumpet, but the bass and the guitar are my main instruments.

As a kid, I studied classical music, so I listened to a lot of it. I also listened to my dad's record collection, which had everything: Miles Davis; Quincy Jones; Joan Armatrading; Jefferson Airplane; Earth Wind and Fire; Crosby, Stills, Nash and Young; Derek & the Dominoes; and so on. Now I am more influenced by bands and singers like R.E.M., U2, Bob Mould, Sarah Mac-Laughlin, Counting Crows, Maria McKee, Luka Bloom, Tracy Chapman and Suzanne Vega.

I performed a lot when I was a young child, but I started playing and singing my own songs at open mics in clubs when I was eighteen. My most memorable performance was opening for Morrissey at Madison Square Garden when I was twenty. I knew that this was my shot. Then I was asked to tour with Morrissey in the U.K.; people wrote to me, and the press called record labels asking about me. Eventually, I signed on to Atlantic Records.

I have not played any lesbian festivals, but I do play at a lot of gay clubs and give performances for AIDS benefits and breast-cancer functions. I don't really know if I have an identity

· ·

Discography

- **Massive Blur**/Atlantic Records, 1993
- **Willing to Wait**/Atlantic Records, 1995
- **Made of Honor** (EP)/ independent, 1996

· ·

Melissa **Ferrick**

as a lesbian musician, but I am definitely "out" — I came out to my family at seventeen. I am not interested in separating myself from the straight world, but I do believe that being a lesbian is a very important part of who I am, and I will continue to struggle for equality.

Right now I'm on a U.S. tour by myself including playing the festival in Monterey over the Labour Day weekend. As well, I just released a new record independently and will continue to write and play for as long as I am physically capable. Besides music, I enjoy good coffee, movies, playing pool, playing golf, and finding time to go on vacations. I am single at the moment, but I am happy to say that I have some wonderful friends in my life.

"I had wanted to play the violin since before I was born."

"I try to be there in the moment with the audience."

I believe that music is eternal and it moves everyone in different ways. It can make sense and then not make sense — there are no rules. It is what makes me happy and fulfilled — not only to give it, but to be a part of receiving it as well. I tend not to try to overtly convey messages to people in my music. I am in the song every time, and I try to be there in the moment with the audience. Honesty and "realness" are the things I think I display.

As for advice, I can really only say this: If music is what is inside your soul, inside your head, inside the insides that you can never explain, then follow it, nurse it, rely on it. Remember that doubt is inevitable, but it is also the easiest emotion to kill. ◄

Fan Fare

Contact
Kelly McCartney, USA;
(310) 394-4394

Website
http://www.hidwater.com/ferrick

Melissa **Ferrick**

Hello Dad

Melissa Ferrick

Hello daddy
Are you drunk again
I've been waiting on the back porch
Waiting to come in
N' good evening daddy
You are asleep again
Lying on the TV couch
With your eyes hid under
Your rim

> *Chorus:*
> But you know that you can't
> You can't fool me
> I know that you still love me
> N' I know that it ain't all of your fault
> You're just a strong headed man
> With a brittle-weak-heart

N' you're waiting, yes you are waiting
For your daddy
'Cause he's going to come and he's going to
Tear you apart
But why can't you hold me
Like the other the other daddies do
And why can't you love me
Like I was a part of you

> *[Chorus]*

Good-bye daddy
Guess that I'll be seeing you around
Because I am old enough to understand
But still too young …
I am just too young …
I am still too young
To know how

> *[Chorus]*

Hello daddy
Are you drunk again
I've been waiting on the back porch
Waiting on the back porch
I am still waiting on the back porch
To come in

© Melissa Ferrick (Nine Two One Music), 1993

M e l i s s a **F e r r i c k**

Ferron

Ferron's work over the past twenty years has been highly praised. She received a four-star review in *Rolling Stone* for *Shadows on a Dime*, and the *New York Times* listed her 1994 release *Driver* as one of the ten best albums of that year (the album was also nominated for a Juno Award). Her recordings have won Ferron a devoted following, even as they have traced a wide arc creatively. As Ferron says, "I realized I must take my life into my own hands to be happy, [and my music shows] the emerging of my soul. The album *Testimony* was a statement that I exist, full of alienation and sarcasm. *Shadows on a Dime* was a study of love and politics."

She followed up that album with *Phantom Center*, a recording in which the singer transcended her folk roots and embraced happiness. Ferron's album, *Resting with the Question*, was a complete departure from what had gone before: it was an instrumental recording full of emotional landscapes. "I had come to the end of my word bank. I was still changing inside; I just went to another place without words," says Ferron. *Not a Still Life* was a live recording from San Francisco's Great American Music Hall, covering sixteen years of songs. *Driver* was lush and quiet and inviting: "It was my way to make music deeper, slower, not being afraid of time passing by, even in the music." As the songs on the 1996 album *Still Riot* attest, Ferron still deals with serious issues — but in an optimistic and uplifting way that "shows how one can overcome anything." ◄

► OPENING NOTES

Date of birth
June 1, 1952

Place of birth
Toronto, ON, Canada

Astrological sign
Gemini

Heritage
French Canadian, Native American

Siblings
Five

Languages
English, some French

Current residence
Vashon, WA, USA

Instruments
Vocals, acoustic guitar, synthesizer

► ► ►

Still Driving

My musical roots are in the folk tradition — singer-songwriters and poetry. Joni Mitchell, Bruce Cockburn and Neil Young were my inspirations. I taught myself to play guitar and began performing when I was a young teen, in the coffee houses of Vancouver, Canada.

I don't really know what makes me want to play music — I love words, and music will just come to me. Sometimes it even wakes me up. Then I just have to write and sing and play the music I have written. I love to hear my music performed with other instruments — so I have to have a band. And then, of course, I want to record it all. Luckily, I have my own band to support my work, both in the studio and in live performance. The band includes my long time guitar player Shelley Jennings; Jami Sieber, who plays electric cello and is an accomplished recording artist herself; Darryl Havers, who plays the keyboards and has co-written several of my new songs; db Benedictson, who plays bass, contributes vocals and is my associate producer and song collaborator; Craig Kaleal, my drummer; and the newest member, Canadian electric guitar player John Ellis.

41

Discography

- **Ferron**/1977 (deleted)
- **Ferron Backed Up**/1978 (deleted)
- **Testimony**/Cherrywood Station, 1980
- **Shadows on a Dime**/Cherrywood Station, 1984
- **Phantom Centre**/Cherrywood Station, 1990
- **Resting with the Question**/Cherrywood Station, 1992
- **Not a Still Life**/Cherrywood Station, 1993
- **Driver**/Earthbeat!, 1994
- **Phantom Centre** (re-release)/Warner Bros. Records/Earthbeat!, 1995
- **Still Riot**/Warner Bros. Records, 1996

F e r r o n

My most memorable performances have been at Carnegie Hall, the Newport Folk Festival and a San Francisco performance that was recorded live. Over the past twenty years, I have also performed at U.S. lesbian music festivals: Michigan, West Coast, Bloomington, Sisterfire. I am an out lesbian — I was never "in" — and am fiercely open as a gay woman. I sing love songs, and I speak to and of women in my songs … But my music is intended to be universal, not exclusive. When

Fan Fare

Publicity
Alisse Kingsley, Warner Bros. Records, 3300 Warner Blvd., Burbank, CA, USA, 91505-4694; (818) 953-3485 (phone) (818) 953-3329 (fax)

Booking agent
Barbara Skydel, Premier Talent Booking, New York, NY, USA; (212) 758-4900

Management
JR Productions, 433 Town Center, Suite 604, Corte Madera, CA, USA, 94925-2022; JRPRODS@aol.com

E-mail fan club
Ferronfan@aol.com

Website
http://ferronweb.com

• • • • • • • • • • • •

"I was never 'in'."

• • • • • • • • • • • •

I'm performing, I'm just trying to have an honest moment with my audience.

These days, I'm inspired by Rickie Lee Jones, Amy Ray and Emily Saliers, as well as the musicians I play with. One highlight in my career was recording my song "Stand Up" (on the *Phantom Center* album) with the Indigo Girls (Amy Ray and Emily Saliers). Working with the Indigo Girls was a blast. It was the first time I had recorded one of my songs with anyone outside of my band. We worked on parts together, including a guitar part for Emily. It was fun, and inspiring and validating for me.

Most recently, I have been working on my first record for Warner Brothers Records. It is entitled *Still Riot* and is scheduled for release in summer/fall 1996. Many stellar musicians and vocalists worked with me on *Still Riot*. My band members and I were joined by Novi Novog (viola) and Larry Tuttle (Chapman Stick), both of whom are

members of Freeway Philharmonic; Lauren Wood (vocals); Vicki Randle (percussion and vocals), who is currently playing on the *Tonight Show*; Scarlet Rivera (violin), who played with Bob Dylan; Emily Saliers of the Indigo Girls (vocals and guitar); and Chris Webster (vocals), who also played on my album *Driver* and has her own recording career. Since I am the producer of *Still Riot*, I had the opportunity to collaborate on arrangments and production, especially with my associate producer, db Benedictson. I also worked with the fine musicians in my band to compose most of the music on the album, which is a "first" for me. It has been the most exhilarating and challenging experience of my career.

Needless to say, I don't really know what "spare time" is. My life is very full. When I am not working, writing, recording, touring and doing interviews, I am having a simple island family life with my little girl and my partner. •

My advice for aspiring lesbian musicians? Tell the truth in your work, whatever the truth may be … and feed the cat! ◀

Ain't Life A Brook

Ferron

I watch you reading a book
I get to thinking our
Love's a polished stone
You give me a long drawn look
I know pretty soon
You're gonna leave our home
And of course I mind
Especially when I'm
Thinking from my heart
But life don't clickety-clack
Down a straight-line track
It comes together and it comes
    apart
You say you hope I'm not the
    kind
To make you feel obliged
To go ticking through your time
With a pained look in your eyes
You give me the furniture
We'll divide the photographs
Go out to dinner one more time
Have ourselves a bottle of wine
And a couple of laughs

When first you left I stayed so sad
I wouldn't sleep
I know love's a gift
I thought yours was mine
And something
That I could keep

Now I realize
Time is not the only compromise
A bird in the hand
Could be an all-night stand
Between a blazing fire
And a pocket of skies
So I hope I'm not the kind
To make you feel obliged
To go ticking through your time
With a pained look in your eyes
I covered the furniture
I framed the photographs
Went out to dinner one more time
Had myself a bottle of wine
And a couple of laughs

Just the other day
I got your letter in the mail
I'm happy for you
It's been so long
You've been wanting
A cabin and a backwoods trail
And I think that's great
Me I seem to find myself in
    school
It's all okay
I just want to say
I'm so relieved
We didn't do it cruel

But ain't life a brook
Just when I get to
Feeling like a polished stone
I get me a long drawn look
It's kind of a drag
To find yourself alone
And sometimes I mind
Especially when I'm
Waiting on your heart
But life don't clickety-clack
Down a straight-line track
It comes together and it comes
    apart
'Cause I know you're not the
    kind
To make me feel obliged
To go ticking through my time
With a pained look in my eyes
I sold the furniture
I put away the photographs
Went out to dinner one last time
Skipped the bottle of wine
And a couple of laughs
For wasn't it fine

JANA BIRCHUM

Girls in the Nose

Formed by Kay Turner and Gretchen Phillips (of Two Nice Girls) in 1985, Girls in the Nose plays raunchy, ribald rock 'n' roll to inspire a lesbocentric vision of peace, love and pussy. The band has travelled nation-wide, recorded two albums and recently produced a video for their song "Breast Exam." They have been featured on DYKE TV and Network Q, have performed at the March on Washington and the Michigan Womyn's Music Festival, and were covered in the *New York Times* and *Curve* magazine. ◄

Clockwise from left: Joanna, Gretchen, Darby, Jean, Kay, Lisa

♪ making music

1985-1987
Kay Turner, vocals; Gretchen Phillips, guitar and vocals; Betsy Peterson, guitar

1987-1990
Kay Turner, lead vocals; Gretchen Phillips, guitar and vocals; Betsy Peterson, guitar; Darcee Douglas, bass; Pam Barger, drums; Joanna Labow, percussion, vocals

1990
Kay Turner, lead vocals; Becky Escamilla, guitar; Karla Thompson, guitar; Darcee Douglas, bass; Terri Lord, drums; Joanna Labow, percussion, vocals

1991-1995
Kay Turner, lead vocals; Lisa Wickware, guitars; MJ Torrance, guitars, piano; Jean DuSablon, bass; Darby Smotherman, drums; Joanna Labow, percussion, keyboard, vocals

With us faithfully from 1988 on: our dancing girls in wigs and poly, Lez Nez (Allison Faust and Kathy Smith)

A Capella (Kay Turner)

The Band That Smells Like a Dyke!

Girls in the Nose (GITN) is a vulva-centric lesbian rock band from deep in the twat of Texas. The band was founded specifically for the purpose of creating music and performance that would define and enhance activist lesbian sexual politics. Herstorically, GITN occupies a middle ground between lesbian singer-songwriter music of the 1970s and out-punk lezzies of the 1990s. In a three-way, we would be doing it with Alix Dobkin and Tribe 8, and we'd be having a blast.

The original group was co-founded by Kay Turner, Gretchen Phillips and Betsy Peterson in 1985 — we three of the big, honking, beautiful noses who actively fantasized about a band of electric dykes heralding a new age of lesbian music. We took our name from our physiognomy. All three of us had been told by men that we would be "prettier" if we got nose jobs. Needless to say, we took this directive and turned it upside down. We

► OPENING NOTES (for the band)

Girls in the Nose is astrologically slanted toward the water signs: the Nose drips. Founders Kay Turner and Gretchen Phillips are both wet — Kay is a Scorpio, born in Detroit, MI, on November 10, 1948, and Gretchen Phillips is a Cancer, born in Houston, TX, on July 19, 1963. Other cosmic swimmers include Cancers Joanna Labow, Lisa Wickware, and MJ Torrance; Pisces Pam Barger and Darby Smotherman; and Scorpio Terri Lord. Bass players Darcee Douglas and Jean DuSablon are both, thank goddess, earth-bound Taurians and we're aired out by Aquarians Becky Escamilla and Betsy Peterson. There is no fire in Girls in the Nose. We prefer flooding.

► ► ►

made our noses into our job: We would be the band that smells like a dyke.

It seems amazing now, but just ten short years ago there were hardly any all-woman electric bands, let alone lezzie electric bands. Certainly we had our predecessors in the 1970s — Deadly Nightshade, ISIS, New Haven Women's Liberation Rock Band — but those bands did not speak consistently and irreverently to dykes about dyke life. We wanted a band that was in your face and in your vulva about sex, sodomy, Sappho, meat, monogamy, Madonna, hips, twats and tits.

Two of us (Kay and Joanna) had been involved in the East Coast lesbian music scene of the 1970s. In 1972, Kay had founded a group in New Jersey called The Oral Tradition. It was a proto-punk glam-trash group whose members bought costumes at K-mart moments before a show, wore black lipstick and generally looked frighteningly fabulous on stage, singing lesbian-reconstituted, pronoun-adjusted a capella covers of straight standards

. . . .

"We mix it up, we play it loud and, every time, we play it proud."

. . . .

such as "Heard It Through the Grapevine" and "California Girls." The Oral Tradition wasn't exactly Olivia Records material. We were brash and

f[...]
c[...]
1[...]
fore[...]
to us[...]

Perhaps [...] for us. It pl[...] that would e[...] to Girls in the [...] pened this way: Kay [...] Texas to get a Ph.D. in folk[...] and there she met the screaming guitar girl of her dreams — a teenaged Gretchen, who worked in a bakery by day and played with a band called Meat Joy by night. We were inevitable. Sitting by the Colorado River in the fall of 1981, half-drunk and fully stoned, we saw a phoenix-shaped cloud rise in the evening sky and knew it was the beginning of something big. We messed around for a couple of years, and then added Betsy, a Pretenders freak who played strange guitar. We finally gave our first show at a party in 1985, where we performed Gretchen's song, "I Spent My Last Ten Dollars on Birth Control and Beer." Our next official gig was in Baltimore at the American Folklore Society's 1986 Annual Meeting. We debuted the song "Menstrual

. . . .

Discography

- **Chant to the Full Moon, Oh Ye Sisters**/Girls in the Nose, 1988
- **Girls in the Nose**/Girls in the Nose, 1990
- **Origin of the World**/Girls in the Nose, 1992
- **Breast Exam** (video)/Girls in the Nose, 1994
- "Weddings Are Icky" on **Outland** (compilation CD)/International Gay and Lesbian Human Rights Commission, 1995

. . . .

...nd ...ull ...er Pam ...arcee ...ging back ...al-pal from New ..., percussionist/vocalist Joanna Labow. We played around Austin during the happy lesbian music moment of the late 1980s. Then Gretchen's other band, Two Nice Girls, got a record deal. Gretchen and Pam left GITN in the fall of 1989 to become famously Nice, and the rest of us took a nose-dive. But not for long.

Three months later, we emerged as a different band with the same mission, tailored for the 1990s. We decided that we wanted to be the house band for Lesbian Nation and spent the next five years writing and performing with only one move, one groove: Dyke Rock.

Our influences range from Sonic Youth to Joni Mitchell, from Scrawl to Madonna to the Pixies. We adore the girls and we take what we can get from the boys and then give it back to the girls. We mix it up, we play it loud and, every time, we play it proud. Over the years, we have played for thousands of women and men, including bald Avengers, middle-aged lesbian lawyers, earnest college boys raised by feminist mothers, angry college girls raised by feminist mothers, dyke bikers in leather, dyke bicyclists in cotton — whoever, wherever. From Seattle to San Francisco to Dallas to Atlanta to New York City to Los Angeles to New Orleans, we have roamed, our noses high in the air, sniffing out dykes.

In addition to album and video production and national tours, highlights of our herstory include playing on the main rally stage for the March on Washington in 1993; playing for several events in celebration of Gay Pride/Stonewall 25 in New York in June 1994; founding and hosting "Lesbopalooza" (a multi-act extravaganza of lesbian pride held annually in June in Manhattan) with the Maul Girls of NYC; being a feature story on DYKE-TV in New York; being filmed in Ellen Spiro's PBS documentary *Greetings from Down Here: Gays and Lesbians in the South*; being interviewed in *Radical Act* by Tex Clark; playing "Breast Exam" in the official video of the March on Washington; and playing at Rhythm-Fest (1990-93), the Lone Star Women's Music Festival (1991-93), the Northampton Lesbian Festival (1992-93) and the Michigan Womyn's Music Festival (1994-95).

As of 1996, the band has taken a break so that members can work on other projects. This may sound like we've broken up — but we haven't, not really. Girls in the Nose will emerge in the late 1990s as a slightly more mature band called Women of the Schnozz. Don't worry, you'll smell us coming! ◄

Fan Fare

Direct orders and other communications
Girls in the Nose,
P.O. Box 49828, Austin, TX,
USA, 78765

Distributor
Ladyslipper Music,
P.O. Box 3124, Durham,
N.C., USA, 27715-3124;
1-800-634-6044

Website
http://www.hidwater.com/
OUTLOUD/gitn.html

More Madonna, Less Jesus

Lyrics: Kay Turner and David Kolwyck
Music: Mary Jo Torrance and Lisa Wickware

Busy your hands,
Busy your hands,
Do the goddess' work
And listen to your glands.
Busy your brain,
Busy your brain,
Get a new religion
Hear this new refrain!

> Chorus:
> More Madonna, Less Jesus
> More Madonna, Less Jesus

In the house of icons
She's tearing down the signs,
Replacing pain with pleasure
Beauty's what you find.
In the church of fathers
Disruption at the core,
When crosses serve as jewelry
And what was less is more

> [Chorus with]
> More Madonna …

In the highest heaven
The blessed Mother roars,
She's coming down to earth again
She's settling the score.
In our holy temple
We know what we stand for,
Doin' drag and feeling fab
On the disco floor

> [Chorus with]
> More Madonna …

Busy your hands,
Busy your hands,
Do the goddess' work
And listen to your glands.
Busy your brain,
Busy your brain,
Get a new religion
Sing this new refrain!

> [Chorus with]
> More Madonna, Less Jesus
> More Madonna, more Madonna, more Madonna …

© Girls in the Nose and Kay Turner, David Kolwyck,
Mary Jo Torrance and Lisa Wickware, 1991

Janis Ian

Throughout her four-decade career, Janis Ian has faced many attempts to sum her up in a sentence or two. The first came in the mid-1960s, when, barely a teenager, she wrote and recorded "Society's Child," about the pressures on a white girl dating a black boy. Although the single became a nation-wide hit, Ian was spat upon at performances and endured shouts of "nigger lover."

In 1973, Roberta Flack had a Top Ten hit with the song "Jesse" from Janis Ian's next album *Stars*. "After that, people stopped calling me a has-been," Ian remembers. She signed with Columbia Records, and her association with that company produced a series of albums that were inventive and critically acclaimed. Her 1975 album *Between the Lines* earned Janis two Grammy awards.

During this era, Janis Ian collaborated with many performers, writers and musical innovators. Then, with a career still on the rise, Ian again did the unexpected: She walked away from it all. "I was turning into an idiot who could only discuss music and business," she says. "I needed to explore some other forms."

In 1992, Ian returned to recording. Her most recent album, *Revenge*, reveals yet another facet of her personality. She still writes about going against the odds but has found new and even more personal insights on love, tenderness and faith. ◄

▶ OPENING NOTES

Date of birth
April 7, 1951

Place of birth
New York City, NY, USA

Astrological sign
Aries

Heritage
Eastern European Jew

Siblings
One brother

Language
English

Current residence
Nashville, TN, USA

Instruments
Vocals, guitar, piano

▶ ▶ ▶

The Best Revenge

Growing up in my particular time and place was lonely but fulfilling. As a child, I had no female role models outside of my immediate family. I didn't know any women who were leading bands, writing songs, playing and singing. There were simply no women doing what I was doing (sad, but true). My first female role model as an artist was the acting teacher Stella Adler, whom I met in 1983, when she was eighty-two and I was thirty-two.

Discography

- **Janis Ian**/Verve/Forecast, 1966
- **A Song for All the Seasons of Your Mind**/Verve/Forecast, 1967
- **The Secret Life of J. Eddy Fink**/Verve/Forecast, 1968
- **Who Really Cares**/Verve/Forecast, 1969
- **Present Company**/Capitol, 1970
- **Stars**/Columbia, 1973
- **Between the Lines**/Columbia, 1975
- **Aftertones**/Columbia, 1976
- **Miracle Row**/Columbia, 1977
- **Janis Ian**/Columbia, 1978
- **Night Rains**/Columbia, 1979
- **Restless Eyes**/Columbia, 1981
- **Falling from Grace "Days Like These"** (F Film)/Polygram, 1992
- **Breaking Silence**/label varies by country, 1993
- **Revenge**/label varies by country, 1995

"I had a succession of really bad teachers."

My musical roots come from the jazz, folk and classical traditions. I learned to play music early. I first played the piano at two and a half years old, when I realized that the sounds my father was making on that instrument

Janis **Ian**

could be taught. I immediately demanded piano lessons and had a succession of really bad teachers. When I discovered the guitar at ten, I learned how to play it on the theory that you couldn't lift a piano, but you could carry a guitar.

I began performing when I was twelve, wherever I could — nursing homes, dorms, clubs, hoots, whatever. Then, when I was fourteen, I wrote "Society's Child" and became well known. My musical inspiration when I was younger came from John Coltrane, Billie Holliday, Nina Simone and Pete Seeger. Today,

Fan Fare

Management
Senior Management, P.O. Box w218200, Nashville, TN, USA, 37221; (615) 646-6767

Booking agent
Fleming Tamulevich, 733/735 N. Main St., Ann Arbor, MI, USA, 48104-1030; (313) 995-9066 (phone); (313) 662-6502 (fax)

Fan club
Janis Ian Subscriber Service, P.O. Box 121797, Nashville, TN, USA, 37212

Hotline
(615) 320-7820

. . . .

"Practise and practise more, rehearse and rehearse more."

. . . .

these musicians still inspire me; I'd also add Ani DiFranco to the list.

My most memorable performance was my worst one, which I won't go into here. Memorable past musical collaborations include one with Chick Corea — need I say more? I'm currently working on an upcoming album with the participation of Ani DiFranco, Chet Atkins and various other musicians. In my spare time (which is scarce), I write columns for *The Advocate* and *Performing Songwriter* magazine, and write my songs. I try to take long walks. My spouse, Patricia, and I go to the movies and giggle.

I think that artists belong to an aristocracy of merit, which is something that I cannot say about any of my other "defining characteristics" (Jew, female, lesbian, second-generation American). As a lesbian, I came out to myself at nine and to my family at twenty. I first came out publicly in 1975, when I was "outed" by the *Village Voice*, and I came out more vocally and publicly in 1992, with the release of my album *Breaking Silence*. I don't perform at lesbian music festivals if I can help it, though. I don't participate as a performer at exclusionary festivals.

The only advice I'd offer an aspiring lesbian musician is the same I'd offer to any musician: practise and practise more, rehearse and rehearse more. That way, when your chance comes, you'll be ready; and knock on doors, bang on walls, go over, under and around them. Trust nothing but your own instinct. Be an artist first, and everything else will follow. ◄

When Angels Cry

Janis Ian

Wait
Your tired arms must rest
Let this moment pass
Wait until the morning
Close your eyes and let me see
who you used to be
Left without a warning
Who knew one so big could grow so small
Lighter than the writing on the wall

    Chorus:
    When angels cry, can I stand by
    When stones weep, can my heart sleep
    Wish I'd never heard
    Wish I'd never heard
    Wish I'd never heard
    The power of a four-letter word

Only love will matter in the end
For a woman or a man
What's the difference now?
Here, we live with bottles
and needles and truth
Here is your living proof
that death cannot be proud
Some say it's a judgement on us all
I can't believe that God could be that small

    [Chorus]

If ever was a soul that longed to fly
If ever was a rose that longed to bloom
If ever was an angel, it was you
So close your eyes and say goodbye
Goodbye

When angels cry, I can't stand by
When stones weep, my heart can't sleep
Guess I've finally learned
Guess I've finally learned
Yes, I've finally learned
Love is just a four letter word
Hope is just a four letter word

J a n i s **I a n**

Nedra Johnson

Nedra Johnson is a Welsh/African-American singer, songwriter and bassist. She comes from a musical family — her mother is a singer-songwriter, and her father, Howard Johnson, is a recording artist who has played with Charles Mingus, Dizzy Gillespie, Jack Dejohnette, Miles Davis, Bob James, Paul Simon, the Band, Phoebe Snow, Gil Evans, Roberta Flack, Donny Hathaway, Taj Mahal and the Saturday Night Live Band. Nedra plays blues, R&B, gospel, funk and rock-inspired music rooted in poetry. Her first full-length album is slated for release in late 1996. ◄

► OPENING NOTES

Date of birth
July 27, 1966

Place of birth
New York, NY, USA

Astrological sign
Leo

Heritage
African-American, Welsh

Siblings
Three brothers

Language
English

Current residence
Brooklyn, NY, USA

Instruments
Vocals, bass, guitar, tuba

The Economics of Grace

I learned to play music in school — in bands and the orchestra. I played alto sax, bari sax, string bass, tuba — and I got an electric bass at age fourteen. I grew up listening to lots of different music. I loved the Jackson 5, Sly and the Family Stone, Jimi Hendrix, Phoebe Snow and Taj Mahal. A little later, I was into Queen, Oingo Boingo, Adam and the Ants, and Culture Club, then Channel 3, Social Distortion and Youth Brigade. I still listen to my old favourites, although I stopped listening to hardcore (punk rock) for a while until the more recent emergence of women's hardcore bands like Tribe 8. Coming out was more like "coming to." It wasn't that I stopped liking the sound of hardcore, I just stopped needing the lyrics or something.

Before I "came to" I was very isolated emotionally, although I was never really closeted. I didn't grow up thinking or fearing I would be a lesbian; I just didn't really understand there were options. I had a short-lived non-sexual relationship with a girl in high school — we kissed and were very close — but it was too difficult to pursue. I asked her if she thought we were gay, and she said, "No." I was relieved. My only idea about possibly being a lesbian was that I'd have to wear work boots. I don't know where that come from, especially because I had no other ideas about lesbian existence.

I finally came out in Woodstock, NY. There was a strong women's community there and I was lucky enough to be mothered and not taken advantage of. I was given books like *Sappho Was a Right-On Woman* and *The Joy of Lesbian Sex*. Up until then, sexuality wasn't really in my consciousness — I was still passively waiting for boys to stop being yucky. Reading *Sappho Was a Right-On Woman* was what really brought me out. It was dated, but I had never identified with anything so strongly — it made everything about me click. I also learned about women's music in Woodstock. The first record I heard was *Lavender Jane Loves Women* by Alix Dobkin. I could dig it.

Discography

■ Album pending

Nedra **Johnson**

My first real gig — meaning the first time I was hired to play — was with Toshi Reagon at the Michigan Womyn's Music Festival. Michigan itself blew me away: The diversity of music at Michigan made me know women's music would be a good place to call home.

I experience the desire to play music as divine, and I think of the music and poetry I grew up with as divine. I would not have survived without it. These days, I am most inspired by poets and writers: Audre Lorde, Pat Parker, Alice Walker and ntozake shange. I have a vision of Audre Lorde marking a path, leaving a trail of poetry and essays — a way out, through, up and over. The other person I must mention as a role model and inspiration is writer/photographer/publisher/teacher/women's music herstorian Toni Armstrong. She has been such an incredible friend throughout my career. She nurtured my vision long before it was really tangible, and her faith is what has kept me going when my own faith was waning.

The feedback that I get after performances has been another source of inspiration. A lot of the time, I feel very isolated in my experiences of the world. I think that my age might have something to do with this — maybe I'm just not seeing myself reflected in anything. It's not so much that I want to be in step with the world; I just wish I knew

· · · · · · · · · · · · · ·

"Black lesbians . . . expressed how moving it was to hear a black woman singing about love . . . toward another woman."

· · · · · · · · · · · · · ·

of more people who were in step with me. After a recent performance, a group of black lesbians came up to me and expressed how moving it was to hear a black woman singing about love, and to know that the love was directed toward another woman. Sometimes I don't even know that something is missing until someone gives me that kind of feedback.

These days, I perform with a band under my own name. Since October 1994, the core of my band has been the "Ladeez in the House" (Debbie Knapper, guitar; Debbie Robinson, bass guitar; Lisette "Peaches" Smith, drums). I do not yet have a permanent keyboard player or rhythm guitarist. Ideally I would have both, as well as a percussionist and horns — but that is a financial issue.

I think it is important to look at lesbian music within the realities of economics. I hear from young women who are frustrated with the women's music that has survived over the last two decades. Yet there were great bands, like the Deadly Nightshade — they were criticized in the women's music community for being electric, and somehow electricity was defined as "patriarchal." Their survival was dependent on a feminist and predominantly lesbian audience. Is that an audience that can hold the interest of (i.e., make money for) a major label? Could an independent women's label in the mid-1970s have afforded the same production values and

N e d r a **J o h n s o n**

distribution as RCA? I don't believe that it is impossible to produce and promote independently with success — Ani DiFranco bears witness to that possibility. She, however, is not a band. She started out touring alone and her records feature her and one other person. My projected recording budget for a full album comes to fifteen thousand dollars — before manufacturing. And then there is the expense of touring. All I can depend upon is listener interest and responsibility.

Right now, I'm preparing to record a four- to five-song extended-play CD. Those songs will then be included on a full-length CD, which I hope to finish in the fall of 1996. The extended-play CD is to be produced by Judith Casselberry. The full CD will be produced by her and

Fan Fare

Promotion/booking agent
Big Mouth Girl Records, P.O. Box 20308, Tompkins Square Station, New York, NY, USA, 10009; (212) 252-2167

E-mail
BIGMGIRL@aol.com

> "I think it is important to look at lesbian music within the realities of economics."

Toshi Reagon. As for my personal life these days, I love a woman whose name is Bob. We've been together for almost four years; I don't know what I'd do without her. She makes everything about my life mo' better and I hope that never changes. And don't even let me *begin* to objectify her … all I can say is that she's all that and a vat of sauce! I joke with her sometimes that she's the "luckiest girl in the world," but I really know that I am.

To aspiring lesbian musicians I say this: The most important thing is to learn to really play your instrument. No one is going to let you play your instrument or play in their band solely because you're a dyke. I certainly would not — for me, the music comes first. This is not to intimidate women starting out: I think

its great to just get hold of an instrument and start a band the same day. That's great! But don't limit yourself. Challenge yourself beyond any one style of music. Listen to everything. Try to play what you hear. Get ready to fill the empty spaces — there is a great shortage of musicians right now. Go to the festivals; you'll see many people sharing band members. Sometimes this is a choice, but often it's because of a lack of choice. Don't be afraid to approach other musicians and ask them what to do. Above all, believe in yourself — and get some understanding of music as a business! ◄

> The most important thing is to learn to really play your instrument."

Nedra **Johnson**

Hail Mary

Nedra Johnson

I was strolling my existence
when I ran into an old friend
from another lifetime.
It was Divine Recognition.
I said, "Welcome Home, baby.
I was sure that you'd be here."
And I wrapped my arms around her.
We said a little prayer.

    First Chorus:
    Hail Mary
    Full of Grace
    Bless this Holy Love we make.
    Bless this Holy Love.

The moon was full in Pisces then,
in the woods on a sacred Land
and I longed to be a farmer
and grow apple trees in Eden.
Touch my Body, move my Will.
I swear that I can see her still.
She is gone
and in the sunset.
She's gone
and in the moon.

    [Repeat first chorus]

Second Chorus:
    Angels sing with the Love we bring!
    Heaven loves what we're made of …
    Bless this Holy Love.

She was an Aries, full and bright.
I am a Leo, waning without her.
My world is Falling.
Hers is Evergreen.
Touch my body, move my Will.
I swear that I can see her still.
In the sunset.
and in the moon.

    *[Repeat first and second
    choruses out]*

© Nedra Johnson, 1991

k.d. lang

k.d. lang is a transcendent artist — a one-woman cultural phenomenon. She began playing guitar at the age of ten and, within three years, was writing and performing her own work. In the early 1980s, k.d. formed her band, the reclines, and quickly drew enthusiastic responses for her stage performances.

Her early records, *Friday Dance Promenade* and *A Truly Western Experience*, were followed by *Angel with a Lariat* which received broad critical acclaim. k.d.'s next album, *Shadowland*, went gold and earned her the Rolling Stone Critic's Pick for Best Female Singer, and Canada's Juno and CASBY awards for Best Female Vocalist of the Year. She won a Grammy for Best Vocal Collaboration for "Crying," her duet with Roy Orbison from the *Hiding Out* sound track album. She also performed on the Canadian leg of the fabled Amnesty International Tour.

Absolute Torch and Twang earned k.d. the Grammy for Best Female Country Vocalist and she was named "Female Artist of the 1980s" by the Canadian Academy of Recording Arts and Sciences. By the early 1990s k.d. was moving boldly into unexplored musical territory with her album *Ingenue*. Co-written by k.d. and long-time associate Ben Mink, *Ingenue*'s ten songs illuminated erotic desire and unrequited love. The album went double platinum in the U.S., won a Grammy and found a whole new audience for the singer. *All You Can Eat* is k.d. lang's most recent album. Recorded with her long-standing core group of musicians, it is the most musically sophisticated of her albums and the definitive work to date. ◄

► OPENING NOTES

Date of birth
November 2, 1961

Place of birth
Edmonton, AB, Canada

Astrological sign
Scorpio

Siblings
One brother, two sisters

Language
English

Current residence
Vancouver, BC, Canada

Instruments
Vocals, guitar, tamboura, mandolin

► ► ►

Fire Walker

I began playing the guitar when I was ten, and by thirteen I was writing and performing my own songs. I feel like I'm second generation lesbian singer. As a sixteen-year-old, I listened to people like Cris Williamson, Meg Christian and Heather Bishop. I saw them as strictly lesbian singers — that's how they were marketed, whether they wanted to be or not. I'm not a big fan of the music business, but my need to create and sing is deeply engrained. I think this is an age-old conflict between the artist and commerce.

Writing and singing songs comes from the need for poetry and to express myself with words — doing my music is innate. I find a lot of inspiration in nature, which has always been a great creative force for me   animals, the way nature works, the weather, trees, birds. I watch crows. They teach me how to dance — that sounds corny, but its true. Just watching the symmetry and collisions within the natural world fascinates me.

Lyrics are very very important to me and I've been inspired by people like Joni Mitchell, Jane Siberry and Leonard Cohen — great song writers, great lyricists, great poets. Musically, Patsy Cline was and is a great influence on me. I also enjoy listening to Bjork, Peggy Lee and Barry White. I like that "fuck-you pop attitude" of British bands like Elastica, Blur and Radiohead. The choruses

Discography

- **Friday Dance Promenade** (7")/Bumstead Records, 1983
- **A Truly Western Experience** (LP)/Bumstead Records, 1984
- **Angel with a Lariat**/Sire, 1986
- **Shadowland**/Sire, 1987
- **Absolute Torch and Twang**/Sire, 1989
- **Ingenue**/Sire, 1992
- **Even Cowgirls Get the Blues** (soundtrack)/Sire, 1993
- **All You Can Eat**/Warner Bros. Records, 1995

k . d . **lang**

in *All You Can Eat* were very influenced by that. I wish I were more alternative. The actual sound and texture of my voice are not alternative, but my mind and my attitude are.

I have an identity as a lesbian musician, but I don't feel political about my preference; I just don't. I feel like it's a part of my life and my sexuality, but it certainly isn't my cause. I'm not a role model — I'm k.d. lang, a singer. I do definitely take a huge amount of pride in being an out lesbian, and having a good section of my audience being gay women at my shows, buying my records and feeling a type of solace in my music and in my persona. At the same time I don't want to be exclusive. I don't want to be a sexist or racist or prejudiced towards other sexualities or other preferences or other listeners who want to interpret it the way they want to interpret it.

When I'm performing, I flirt with my audience because they're my lovers. Being a singer is so all-encompassing that you have to acknowledge your sexuality and sensuality, charisma and anxiety. I have to be honest when I'm up there. When I came out

"The symmetry and collisions within the natural world fascinate me."

on the *Ingenue* tour, I would open the song "Miss Chatelaine" by saying, "Yes, the rumours are all true. It's time I told you: I am a L-L-Lawrence Welk fan." I threw that Lawrence Welk thing in there because I didn't want to get onstage and say, "Isn't it great that I'm a lesbian?" but I wanted to acknowledge it in a funny way that wouldn't alienate the straight people who were there strictly because I'm a musician.

Lesbianism, as we know it, is an extremely diverse culture; I feel it is hard to confine it to one type of culture. The alternative nature of being gay or being a lesbian is something that we should pride ourselves on. Don't look at it as a negative thing or an obstacle. Look at it as a celebratory difference; something that we can utilize in a fashion that sets us apart,

that may give us a slightly different take on the world. But I also don't think we should exploit our sexuality whether we're straight or gay or whatever we're into. I think it's something that we should treat with as much reverence as anything else.

I've been criticized by people who think I came out in order to gain publicity, which is completely wrong. Satisfying the public is a very tricky subject. I've been very conscious about doing enough gay press but not alienating the straight press. It's very difficult to balance because it's relatively new territory — mass circulation gay publications like *Out* and *The Advocate* as well as big names coming out as lesbians in the mainstream media. The whole lesbian chic thing has really changed how we are covered in the press, but I don't think anyone can be particularly objective about it or have any sort of overview — it's tricky when you have any minority in the public eye.

All my life I've known I would be and have wanted to be famous, to have a hit record … and with *Ingenue* I got it. It's

k . d .   **lang**

not unlike wanting to smoke opium. You smoke it; the high is fantastic. But then there's the down, and then there's the vacuum that you enter that makes you want it more. The title of my last album, *All You Can Eat*, was a commentary on the options in life and how you choose to nourish yourself. It's about never being satisfied with what you're getting; about the whole endless hunger that we feel.

These days I'm still travelling to L.A., but I'm based in Vancouver. I was living in Los Angeles, and things were headed for a crash when something snapped and I realized that I don't belong there. So I pulled myself out. I don't feel comfortable there. It's no different from living in Consort, Alberta — everyone knows everything about

· · · · · · · · · · ·

"A good record . . . has to be something you can fuck to, cook to, listen to and drive to."

· · · · · · · · · · ·

everybody. There's no privacy, no security, nothing sacred, no loyalty. Maybe I'm overly sensitive, or maybe I'm a crazy, eccentric kook who lives in her own world; if I am, then so be it! When I got back to Vancouver, I found that my old friends, whom I've known for twelve years, loved me just the same, even though I hadn't been around for five years. It was like finding a huge refuge. I had to get myself together, because, ultimately, I'm a small-town Canadian girl. I've been on the road for a year so I really don't know where I live at this point! After this latest tour ends I have absolutely no plans, which feels fantastic.

Why do I do what I do? When I'm singing there are moments when I am truly not in control; they are completely just passing through me. I just open up and let the music channel through me. Those are the best deliveries. I want to deliver honesty — pure honest emotion. And when I record my songs, my criteria for making a good record is that it has to be something you can fuck to, something you can cook to, something you can listen to in the morning, and something you can drive to. If

Fan Fare

Management
Bumstead Productions, P.O. Box 110, Hoboken, NJ, USA, 07030-0110; (201) 659-4700 (phone); (201) 659-4006 (fax); lww@bumstead.com (e-mail)

Fan club
Obvious Gossip, P.O. Box 33800, Station D, Vancouver, BC, Canada, V6J 5C7

Website
http://www.infohouse.com/obviousgossip/

you can do all those things to an album, it's a good album!

As for advice, I guess the only thing I can say is that I don't think you're ever free of trials of faith — every day you're faced with one, no matter how small the size of it. Personally, I feel like I am so alone in this world right now. Sometimes I feel like I'm the only vegetarian left, the only vegan in the world left. I feel like all the lesbians are starting to fuck men, and all the straight girls want to be lesbians. So my new motto is this: Emulate those fire-walkers who walk on hot coals. ◄

Hot Pick

Constant Craving

k.d. lang and Ben Mink

Even through the darkest phase
Be it thick or thin
Always someone marches brave
Here beneath my skin

> *First Chorus:*
> Constant craving
> Has always been

Maybe a great magnet pulls
All souls towards truth
Or maybe it is life itself
That feeds wisdom
To its youth

> *[Repeat first chorus]*

Second Chorus:
Craving
Ah ha
Constant craving
Has always been

[Repeat first chorus twice]

[Repeat second chorus once]

[Out with:]
Has always been

© PolyGram/Bumstead, 1992

Connie Lofton

Connie Lofton is a singer/songwriter/guitarist who performs a highly energetic, unique combination of original blues, rock and country music. Her powerful vocals and penetrating songs have attracted a loyal following in her home city of New York, particularly within the gay community. She also recently performed two sets at the National Women's Music Festival and appeared at several regional women's music events. She is a member of Out-Music, the national gay/lesbian musicians' collective.

In early 1996, Connie released her first album, *With My Luck ...*, a ten-track collection of songs "for the lesbian in everyone," which she wrote, performed, produced and engineered. As the New York Native raved, Connie "plays hot, nasty, jangly guitar. From the moment she launches her tasty walking bass-line intros, your feet cannot resist the beat. She's got a strong voice, perfect for growling her own good-time rock and roll songs ... A fine musical talent." ◄

► OPENING NOTES

Date of birth
July 15, 1964

Place of birth
Chicago, IL, USA

Astrological sign
Cancer

Heritage
African-American

Siblings
Two older brothers

Language
English

Current residence
New York City, NY, USA

Instruments
Vocals, guitar, piano, bass, drum machine

► ► ►

A Black Chick Plays the Beatles

I've been playing music for about twenty-six years. I've always had a pretty decent ear and was able to pick out simple tunes on the piano when I was about three or four. I took piano lessons from the time I was five until I was about eleven or twelve, but then I switched to guitar as I thought it was much sexier.

I grew up listening to late 1960s rock, Motown, and the Top 40. As I reached my teens, I became interested primarily in rock 'n' roll (anything from the 1950s on), although now I do listen to blues, R&B and traditional country. Growing up, my female role models were my mom, Julie Andrews, Ronnie Spector, Diana Rigg, Nadia Comaneci and Billie Jean King. However, the Beatles are my musical inspiration, first and foremost. It's almost impossible to for me to imagine that I'd do what I do, or even listen to the music I listen to, if not for those guys. It's not even that my stuff sounds like theirs; they just gave (and still give) me the passion. Besides, they were among the first people who made it respectable for you to just go out and learn to play on your own — you could just get together with mates, make some noise and possibly get famous. Oh, and meeting girls didn't hurt, either — who wouldn't want that?

I performed at piano recitals when I was a kid, but my first performance as a guitar-player/singer was at a Beatles convention in downtown Chicago when I was sixteen. My friend and I entered the "sound-alike" contest and came in second or third. It was quite exciting, and terrifying as well because the crowd was one of the biggest (maybe 2,000 people) I'd performed for, and, as you can imagine, it was quite a shock for some white suburban Beatles

Discography

- **With My Luck** ... /Single Pigeon, 1996

Connie **Lofton**

fans to see this black chick trying to sound like Paul McCartney!

My most memorable "public" performance was at last year's Gay Pride Parade music stage in New York — it was just a great vibe all around. I'd have to say, however, that the most memorable performance I've ever given was at a memorial service for my friend Dean, who died of AIDS about three years ago. His lover wanted me to sing "Running Up That Hill" by Kate Bush; it was one of Dean's favourites and a song I frequently do as part of my set. I was crying through the whole thing — while I was singing, the lyrics took on a particular poignancy because of the occasion. I was wiped out for hours afterwards.

I've performed at several U.S. lesbian music festivals: Campfest in Pennsylvania (1995 and 1996) and the National Womyn's Music Festival in Bloomington, Indiana (1996). I feel that I have an identity as a "lesbian musician" only because I'm a lesbian and I play music. I addressed "lesbian" issues when I first came out at college in 1988, but that's not as important to me anymore. I

"I don't feel complete if I'm not either playing or listening to music."

admit that I want as many people as possible to listen to my songs, and I don't feel the need to single out one group of listeners because of what pronoun I happen to use in a lyric. I don't think it would be too difficult for someone looking at me to figure out what my story is, so I don't feel like I'm hiding anything.

These days, I'm mainly focusing on writing more songs and performing, but I hope to start working on a second album by late fall. In what little spare time I have, I normally listen to music or write. I also spend some time on the computer. I have lots of good friends and my life-partner, soul-mate, significant other, angel love, Jennifer — my girlfriend of four years.

My approach to music is simply this: I don't feel "complete" if I'm not either playing or listening to

music. It is something that I have to do, both physically and emotionally. The musicians I gravitate toward today are doing something I'd like to be doing, either because of their of raw emotional honesty (Nirvana, Hole, Alanis Morrisette, Tori Amos), or brilliant songwriting skills (Kirsty MacColl, Elvis Costello, Mary Chapin Carpenter). Anyone who has stuck by their guns and managed to keep doing music on their own terms, regardless of their level of success, is an inspiration.

It sounds hokey, but the advice I'd offer to aspiring lesbian musicians is just to be true to yourself. Plug into the existing women's music scene wherever you are and however you can, and just play whenever possible! Oh yeah — and you can never have too many gloves, hats, or shoes. Cheers! ◀

Fan Fare

Promotion/booking agent/fan club
C. Lofton, c/o Single Pigeon Productions, P.O. Box 1728, New York, NY, USA, 10159-1728

Connie **Lofton**

Escape

Connie Lofton

I've got my ticket — my bags are packed
It's finally come to this and there ain't no looking
  back
Won't you help me mister, point me towards the
  gate
My destiny is waiting, you know I can't be late
I'm on the run tonight, I've finally been set free
Don't bother coming for me, you won't find me

I still don't understand all I've been through
Spent seven years caught up living through hell with
  you
My friends said get out girl, get out while you can
But when you've been beat down so long, it's hard
  to take a stand
But I'm on the run tonight, I've finally been set free
Don't bother coming for me, boy — you won't find
  me

Married at sixteen, defeated by twenty-one
Up to that time I'd never felt important to anyone
  but you
And you took advantage, you made me blind
I trusted in love, I trusted in God's good graces
So I put up with the fights, I put up with the slaps to
  my face
I put up with everything to be by your side
But I couldn't face their questions, there was
  nowhere I could hide
And after years of practice, I soon believed the lies

But a look in the mirror made me see the truth
A battered, tear-stained face — the legacy of you
It's gonna take a long time to get myself through this
But I'm taking the first step to reclaim the life I've
  missed

Yeah, I'm on the run tonight, I've finally been set free
Don't bother coming for me, boy — you won't find me

I lay me down, let my thoughts stray
And let these blessed engines carry me far away
I packed my bags — left no note goodbye
Will you even notice, baby — will I finally make you
  cry
Will a little hurt from me make you see what you've
  done

Or will you turn your rage on some unsuspecting one

But it's just me now, me is all I've got

And that might not be much, but it just might be a lot
Don't know if I can make it, but I've got to try
This little bird has got to fly
Got to fly

© C. Lofton/BMI, 1995

Faith Nolan

Faith Nolan's political work is her music — her songs are strongly rooted in her working-class African-Canadian heritage and in her commitment to social justice. She is an accomplished musician who plays slide guitar, tambourine and harmonica in styles that vary from blues to folk, from jazz to funk and reggae, while her silky voice wraps itself around songs about Black history and heritage, feminism and working-class struggle. Faith has given stirring and acclaimed performances at universities, unions, music festivals, picket lines and women's prisons in her quest to expose poverty, racism and violence against women, and bring about social change. She is that rare artist: one who can move her audience with music, while allowing her song's message to ring out loud and clear. ◄

► OPENING NOTES

Date of birth
February 6, 1957

Place of birth
Halifax, NS, Canada

Astrological sign
Aquarius

Race
Black, Native/Micmac, South Asian, White

Culture
Black/Afro-Nova Scotian/ Cape Breton Irish

Siblings
One sister, two half-brothers

Language
English

Current residence
Burnt River, ON, Canada

Instruments
Vocals, acoustic lead/rhythm guitar, harmonica, tamborine

► ► ►

The Emotional Renderings of Sound

From the age of three, I was raised in the Afro-Nova Scotian community in Toronto, Ontario. I now live in the woods in a small Ontario community called Burnt River, in a house I built myself.

I grew up hearing calypso, Ella Fitzgerald and church music. I fell in love with blues and folk at the age of twelve. By fourteen, I was a soloist in church. When I was growing up, our home was always full of "Scotians" — and cards, craps and liquor — on the weekends. We kids would play outside or in our rooms. As a young person in the 1960s, I was influenced by the Black Power Movement, the Women's Movement, the Lesbian and Gay Movement and the Peace Movement. My mother, who was strong, independent and full of fire, became my foremost female role model.

I came out as a lesbian at twelve years old — which was also when I had my first sexual relationship — and I have never looked back. I am out as a

> "Music must uplift the oppressed and become a cultural tool."

Discography

- **Rainbow Woman**/Multicultural Womyn in Concert(MWIC), 1984
- **Black Heritage Through Music**/MWIC, 1985
- **Africville**/MWIC, 1986
- **Sistership**/MWIC, 1987
- **Freedom to Love**/MWIC, 1989
- **Hard to Imagine**/MWIC, 1995

Faith **Nolan**

lesbian musician because to hide being a lesbian would be to live a lie and to have a shame-filled and pain-filled existence. I want to emancipate lesbians through music — just as I want to eliminate classism, racism and sexism through my art — so that I can live a proud and dignified life, the kind of life every human being has a right to.

I have played professionally (in other words, made a living from my music) for nineteen years. When I was younger, I was inspired by Odetta, Bessie Smith, Nellie Lutcher, Carmen Mac-Crae and Phoebe Snow. They all inspire me still, along with Judy Collins, Buffy Sainte-Marie, Elizabeth Cotton, Odetta, Memphis Minnie and Abby Lincoln. Highlights of my career include playing with Odetta and with Elizabeth Cotton, opening for Angela Davis, Oliver Tambu (ANC) and Rigoberta Menchu, and going on tour in Japan and Denmark.

· · · · · · · · · · · · ·

"To hide being a lesbian would be to live a lie."

· · · · · · · · · · · · ·

Today, I occasionally gig with band musicians Rachel Melas (bass), Barb Taylor (bass), Sherri Shute (guitar) and Assar Santanna (congos). Every day, like every musician, I work on learning more chords and I practise scales and voicing. I am also composing a jazz album and have some new bluesy/ folky tunes on the go. In my spare time, I do carpentry and I garden, read and play lots of different games. I spend as much time as I can with my special chosen family partners: Dionne, Melanie, Faith Jr., Willi, Jordon, Barb, Filomena, Anadan and Angela.

· · · · · · · · · · · · ·

"My mother was strong, independent and full of fire."

· · · · · · · · · · · · ·

I play music because I love the emotional renderings of sound. My musical philosophy is this: Music must uplift the oppressed and become a cultural tool that helps us not only to survive, but to better ourselves and the world. I believe that we should not compromise ourselves as people of colour, working-class people and lesbians, because these are the things that what will carry us through to live honest, dignified lives. My advice to aspiring musicians is this: Play and sing what you believe and feel, and carry us with you. ◄

Fan Fare

Promotion
MWIC, P.O. Box 690, Station P, Toronto, ON, Canada, M5S 2Y4; (416) 537-8194

Faith **Nolan**

Hot Pick

Little Girl Blue

Faith Nolan

There you sit,
braids in your hair,
scuffed-up sneakers,
a hole in your clothes somewhere.

Not safe to laugh or cry,
nobody asks you why,
feel like you want to die,
little girl blue.

   Chorus:
   Little girl blue,
   I'm just like you,
    come and fly, my, little girl blue.

Some say you're special,
the best of both worlds,
neither black nor white,
most times you don't seem real.

The mirror tells no lie,
look close and see,
open up your eyes,
you're black just like me.

   [Chorus]

This lonely race,
with a lie for a name,
leaves you so displaced,
can't you see we're all the same.

Little girl blue,
become a womon now,
love your people, love your self,
that's the way how.

   [Chorus]

© Faith Nolan, 1992

Faith **Nolan**

Geneviève Paris

Geneviève Paris is an exceptional artist — one who possesses a rare and versatile talent that lends itself equally to classical and rock music. Influenced by classical, folk and rock music, the seventeen-year old Paris launched herself on the French popular music scene and, at eighteen, released her first album of original songs.

While still barely in her twenties, Paris toured extensively across Europe and Quebec, Canada, and released her critically acclaimed second album, *Entre le vert et le gris*. She fell in love with Quebec and moved there permanently in 1983, where she worked as a guitarist, pianist and composer, learned the synthesizer, arranged music, taught at Concordia University and starred in the musical comedy *La Saga du Golfe*.

In 1985, Paris began an extensive, two-year tour — this time as a solo artist playing acoustic guitar and piano. Her fifth album, *Miroirs*, was listed among the top three albums of 1990 by the Quebec newspaper, *La Presse*. Most recently, Paris has worked on the rock opera *Sand et les Romantiques* and participated in numerous collaborations and musical events. Her biography will be published by VLB Éditeurs in Quebec this year. Her sixth album, *Sixième sens*, like all her work, demonstrates the talents of an accomplished and sophisticated artist whose polished melodies offer a unique perspective on the universal themes of love and many kinds of relationships. ◄

▶ OPENING NOTES

Date of birth
September 7, 1956

Place of birth
Paris, France

Astrological sign
Virgo

Heritage
"I have not inherited anything yet."

Siblings
One brother

Languages
French, English, Spanish, a little Russian & Latin

Current residence
Montreal, QC, Canada

Instruments
Vocals, classical & electric guitar, piano, synthesizer

▶ ▶ ▶

Creating a Very Particular Feeling

I was raised in a "Parisian bourgeoisie" family of teachers and college directors. My father was an architect. My female role models in life came from my family — it was full of headstrong women. I was different in my interests — I was into drawing, writing and playing music. I don't remember having had an easy childhood. Maybe that is why I emigrated to Canada.

I learned to play music quite early in life. Actually, as long as I can remember, I have felt that I was born to be a musician. When I was a child, I would visit a friend of my mother's who had a grand piano. I would spend whole afternoons at the piano — not playing, but listening very carefully to the sound and harmonics of each note, and then two notes and three together, and so on. I started learning classical guitar at thirteen, and, at seventeen, I won first prize in that instrument at the International Conservatory of Paris.

I don't remember my very first performance (neither in love nor music!). I know I started to play in folk clubs in Paris when I was fifteen. My most memorable gig was my first "professional" appearance in Bordeaux, France. I was eighteen and

Discography

- **11 chansons**/Disc'Az., 1976
- **Entre le vert et le gris**/Disc'Az., 1978
- **Boulevard du crime**/Disc'Az., 1979
- **Achevez-moi**/Disc'Az., 1982
- **Miroirs**/Audiogram, 1990
- **Sixième sens**/Audiogram, 1995

there were eight thousand people in front of me. This was my first lesson in how to be a good performer in front of a crowd!

What makes me want to play music? Well, I don't "want" to … I have to. I want to elevate

· · · · · · · · · · · · · · ·

"Lesbianism, like music, is not an involvement — it's a state of being."

· · · · · · · · · · · · · · ·

people through my music. I try to help others understand the spiritual force that I feel. I am looking for a "very particular feeling" in my writing process, and for that reason, music has inspired me more than individual musicians themselves. I have taken a little bit of this and that from here and there — in particular, I have been inspired by the first movement of Frank's symphony in D minor, the first Shumann concerto for piano in A minor, and the Berlioz symphony. I love almost everything about all forms of art between

the two World Wars. When I studied classical guitar, I played a lot of South-American composers such as Villa-Lobos, Lauro and Gismonti. I think that when they wrote for guitar they had a real comprehension of the instrument.

I do not feel that I have an identity as a "lesbian musician." I hope there is a bit more than that to my identity! I have never performed at a lesbian festival (although I have played in lesbian clubs here in Quebec). I have, however, come out as a lesbian in my music, especially on my last album. I also worked like crazy on the five previous albums not to say "he" instead of "she." Actually, I may have made it more explicit on my last album because of the fatigue of doing that.

I do love to play or sing with my colleagues, and past musical collaborations include: Maxime Le Forestier and Julien Clerc (in France); Michel Rivard (in Paris as well as here in Quebec); and Richard Séguin, Sylvie Tremblay and Jim Corcoran in Quebec. Currently, I have no plans except to go further with my work.

My advice to aspiring lesbian musicians is: Work! Being lesbian means that, against all odds, we have to believe in ourselves and remain assured that we are normal and well-balanced and that we are absolutely right to choose to

· · · · · · · · · · · · · · ·

"I felt that I was born to be a musician."

· · · · · · · · · · · · · · ·

be who we are. Then we have to lead our lives accordingly. The same thing happens with music. Lesbianism, like music, is not an involvement — it's a state of being. ◄

Fan Fare

Promotion/booking agent
Pascale Graham, 294 Carré St-Louis, bureau 106, Montreal, QC, Canada, H2X 1A4; (514) 849-7848 (phone); (514) 849-6037 (fax)

Website
http://www.audiogram.com/artiste/paris/paris.html

Geneviève **Paris**

Dessine-moi une chanson

Geneviève Paris

Rêve et chante pour nous encore
Aide-nous à apprendre à vivre
Ouvre tes ailes, tu t'envoles
Et tu reviendras nous dire
Ce qu'il y a là-bas

Il y a des montagnes et des dunes
Des pages, des plages immenses
Des soleils et des lunes
Des ciels, des reves d'enfance

Pur, comme l'eau qui nous manque
Un ange se pose sans bruit sur le sable

Seul sur mon étoile
J'ai tout, j'ai rien
J'attends en vain
Seul je lève les voiles
Je viens au monde enfin
Mon bateau s'échouera
Je m'en irai demain
Mais je me souviendrai
De tout, de toi, de vous, de nous

Un voyage sans autre bagage qu'une image
Un cadeau, un secret, un lien entre toi et moi

Viendrez-vous me voir
Tous les jours
Mon amie, mon amour
Viendras-tu t'asseoir
A côté de moi
A la tombée du jour
Prendre soin des roses
Qui meurent chaque soir
De manque d'amour
De manque d'espoir

Un ange tombe sans bruit sur le sable
Une étoile s'embrase dans le ciel de nuit
Un ange tombe sans bruit sur le sable
Sur la terre éphémère, après la mort, la vie …

Dream Our Song

[English Translation by Zoe Welch]

Dream our song for us again
Teach us to live
Spread your wings, fly
And return to tell us
What lies beyond

I've seen mountains and sand dunes,
open pages and wide beaches,
of suns and moons,
of skies and the dreams of our youth

Pure, like a first drink of water,
An angel lands without sound upon the sand

Alone on my star
I have everything and nothing,
waiting in vain.
Alone, I raise the sail
and enter the world at last.
My vessel will find its shore.
Tomorrow, I'll be gone
But I'll remember everything —
you, all of you, us

I'll go with nothing but a vision,
a gift, a secret, a tie that binds us

Will you come and see me
every day
my friend, my love?
Will you sit beside me
as the day closes?
Take care of the roses
that die each night
from lack of love
and loss of hope

An angel falls without sound upon the sand
A star sets fire to the night sky
An angel falls without sound upon the sand,
upon this fleeting earth,
and after death: life.

© Geneviève Paris/Calligram, 1995

Geneviève **Paris**

Phranc

Singer-songwriter Phranc is known as a surfer-dyke supreme, a folkster with attitude and the All-American Jewish Lesbian Folksinger." *Goofy Foot*, Phranc's 1995 EP, was her first lengthy recording in three years ("I was busy surfing, swimming and working on my visual art — my cardboard sculptures," explains Phranc), and demonstrates her versatility and eclectic interests. The EP features the talents of Hole's Patty Schemel and Bikini Kill's Tobi Vail, and includes three new Phranc tunes as well as covers of several pop classics. The title track on *Goofy Foot* is an original instrumental that features "classic" surf instrumentals, says Phranc, who has been "hanging 10" since the age of nine. ◄

OPENING NOTES

Date of birth
August 28, 1957

Place of birth
Santa Monica, CA, USA

Astrological sign
Virgo

Heritage
Jewish

Languages
English, a little Hebrew

Current residence
Santa Monica, CA, USA

Instruments
Vocals, guitar

▶ ▶ ▶

Discography

- **Folksinger**/Rhino, 1985
- **I Enjoy Being a Girl**/Island, 1989
- **Positively Phranc**/Island, 1991
- **Phranc Bulldagger Swagger; Hillary's Eyebrows** (7")/Kill Rock Stars, 1994
- **Goofy Foot** (EP)/Kill Rock Stars, 1995

Being Phranc and Visible

Both of my grand-fathers played guitar and violin, and I played violin myself when I was very young. I started taking guitar lessons at nine years of age. My biggest musical influences were Allan Sherman and Alix Dobkin. Alix and the lesbian writer and activist Jill Johnston changed my life — through them, I knew I wasn't the only lesbian in the world.

I am currently working on a project entitled "Phranc 'n' Stein." It involves me collaborating with two other lesbian musicians to write music for selections from Gertrude Stein's book *Tender Buttons.*

"I come out as a lesbian every time I perform on stage."

I definitely have a "lesbian musician identity," and have been out in every aspect of my life. In fact, I am known as the "All-American Jewish Lesbian Folksinger." Over the years, I have performed at women's music events such as the Michigan Womyn's Music Festival and Wimminfest in New Mexico, and I come out as a lesbian every time I perform on stage. I think it is important for me to be out on stage because, when I was coming out, I found it hard to find other visible lesbians. In general, I try to take my music to as many young people as possible. ◄

Fan Fare

Booking/info
(310) 453-6337 (phone/fax, in the USA)

Fan club
Phranc Phans, 1653 18th Street #2, Santa Monica, CA, USA, 90404

85

Dress Code
Phranc

Don't tell me what to do
Don't tell me what to say
Don't tell me what to wear
Or how to cut my hair
Don't lay your dress code on me

Chorus:
You don't have to prick me I bleed anyway
No you don't have to prick me I bleed anyway

Don't tell me
What to draw, what to paint
Who to sleep with, what to think
What to film, what to see
What to watch, who I can be
Who to talk to, what to eat
What to read, what to write
What I want, what I need
How to look, who I can be
Don't lay your morality on me

And you don't have to prick me
I bleed anyway

Because I'm a woman
Because I know who I am
And I'm out spoken and say that I'm a lesbian
Because I'm brave and I don't lie
Because I'm pink inside

[Repeat chorus]

So don't tell me what to do
Don't tell me what to say
Don't tell me what to wear
Or how to cut my hair
Don't lay your dress code on me

P h r a n c

Random Order

Random Order is hard to classify: Imagine a sound that starts with the slow rhythm of reggae and builds to a pulse with rock and ska, adds a dash of hip-hop and a pinch of blues funk, and spices it all up with a hint of cajun and calypso. Imagine this music played by a band with three lesbians at its centre. Imagine this, and you would discover Random Order.

Formed in 1989, the Toronto, Ontario band has undergone several transformations, has traveled extensively in Southern Ontario and the mid-western States and is particularly renowned among loyal fans in the gay community for its energetic live shows. As bassist Rachel Melas explains, "We don't want to be pigeonholed, but we do love playing to our own communities!" ◄

making music

Rachel Melas
Bass

Conny Nowe
Drums

S. Lynn Phillips
Vocals, guitar, trumpet, drums

Discography

- **Destiny**/independent release, 1990
- **A Giant Leap of Faith**/independent release (compilation CD), 1991
- **Soul Control**/independent release, 1993
- **Wired For Sound**/independent release (CKLN compilation CD), 1994
- **Not a Perfect World**/independent release, 1996

Note: The first two recordings were with original Random Order members Audrey Van Bolhuis and Lynn Payne, now of Tribe 8.

A Capella (S. Lynn Phillips)

The Sweet Music of Diversity

I was born on August 15, which makes me a true-blue Leo — we're talking limelight Leo! I love performing, particularly for an audience that includes dykes!

My musical roots are diverse. At home, I heard country, calypso, classical, opera, Motown and Acid Rock. For instance, at the age of seven I was listening to the Supremes and simultaneously rocking out with Jimi Hendrix! My primary female role model when I was growing up was Christie Love. I admired her because she was a tough cop who knew karate. I even took karate myself. Years later, my mother ruined this fantasy of mine when she showed me a newspaper article stating that Christie is a Jehovah's Witness. I was really disappointed. Other than Christie, women in music were my role models — women such as Joan Armatrading and Chrissie Hynde. I was also inspired by Phoebe Snow, Jimi Hendrix and Janis Joplin.

Left to right: Lynn, Rachel, Conny

▶ **OPENING NOTES**
(S. Lynn Phillips)

Date of birth
August 15 — "I don't do birth years."

Place of birth
Glace Bay, NS, Canada

Astrological sign
Leo

Siblings
Two brothers, one sister

Language
English

Current residence
Toronto, ON, Canada

▶ ▶ ▶

> **"An atmosphere of genuine creativity transpired into some very enthusiastic live performances."**

I have been playing music all my life. I began singing at an early age and my school report cards always stated that I had a good voice and talked too much! When I was seven, a representative from the Ontario Conservatory showed up at our door and asked my mother if I was interested in taking lessons. The representative was a good salesperson and talked me into taking Hawaiian steel guitar (lap steel). In fact, my first musical performance was as part of an ensemble of steel guitars, at the age of ten. By that time, however, I had realized that the only kind of music I would learn was Hawaiian and country (arrgh!) and I promptly quit. I decided that if I was going to be a rock star I would have to

change over to "normal" guitar. My father found me a private tutor, and the tutor taught me how to play the songs I really wanted to play — like "Going to the Chapel" and "Smoke on the Water."

Around the age of twelve, my brother Russ, who was in a rock band, taught me to play drums. I am grateful to my family for encouraging me in music and am thankful that my parents paid for my guitar lessons. My siblings, particularly Russ, have always been supportive, too. I mention this because so many musicians are not taken seriously by their families and peers.

> **"Music . . . is a way to synthesize my political, personal and fictional ideas."**

The first generation of Random Order met at Toronto's Lesbian and Gay Pride Day in 1989.

When we first got together, we inspired one another because we were all fairly new to playing in a band and did not have any formal training. This resulted in an atmosphere of genuine creativity that transpired into some very enthusiastic live performances.

Nowadays, I am the only original remaining member and my current bandmates are a good combination of the technically adept and creatively adventurous. This results in a tight, professional, yet very entertaining and fun band. There are five members in the band: three dykes, one fag and one straight male — Imre Geiszt on accordion and John Jowett on trombone. (We often do shows without the male contingent, or replace them with women at events that require all-women performers. I am comfortable with this arrangement.)

I have a "lesbian musician" identity in that audience members are certainly aware that I am a lesbian. I don't think about it too much because it is so ingrained in my soul that it is an obvious part of me (I came out early — to myself when I was fourteen and had a relationship

> "It is important to see that dykes and fags are represented in the music industry."

with a young woman who was sixteen, and officially to the rest of the world when I was eighteen).

Our most memorable performances were at Lesbopalooza in New York City, 1995; and at the Toronto Lesbian and Gay Pride Day, 1990 through 1996. Performing at these events is exhilarating — it is exciting to look out into the audience and see dykes, fags and heteros together. It is also encouraging to see so many people enjoying our music. I think it is important

for younger musicians, and young people in general, to see that dykes and fags are represented in the music industry.

These days, I am inspired musically by Bob Marley, Tracy Chapman's latest release, Jimmy Scott, Bessie Smith, Big Mama Thornton, Prince and Run DMC. In addition to my performing, I teach guitar at three community schools. I have been doing this job for twelve years and enjoy it, but would like to give it up soon, as I want to dedicate more time to performing, touring, writing and recording.

I play music because it allows me to put forth both my political beliefs and my day-to-day living experiences. It is a way to synthesize my political, personal and fictional ideas into a musical and lyrical arrangement — a song. And it makes me very happy! My advice to aspiring

dyke musicians is: Make sure you are having fun, be true to yourself and your beliefs, and be flexible. Make some clear short-term and long-term goals — for instance: Plan how many songs you will write in a certain period of time and when you will record them. Try to develop a sense of how you want to be presented and the direction in which you want your music to take you. If you are collaborating on a project or working with a band, communicate clearly and ask others to do the same. This will save you time and frustration. Do not assume that everyone is playing for the same reasons as you are and that everyone shares the same goals. Find out simply by asking, and decide what you will and can work with. Try to maintain a professional attitude, and only accept and give constructive criticism. And remember: Enjoy what you're doing — it will show in your work. ◄

91

Fan Fare

Promotion/booking agent/fan club
Random Order, P.O. Box 243, Station E, Toronto, ON, Canada, M6H 2XO; (416) 658-4517

Hot Pick

Oppression

Lyrics: S. Lynn Phillips
Music: Random Order

When you tell me
apartheid don't exist
then I'll tell you
I'm glad to hear it
but when you tell me
sexism still around
then I'll tell you
how many times
do I have to say

> *Chorus [repeat four times]:*
> Oppression is oppression

You can paint it with colour
you can divide it by class
you can say there is a weaker sex
and then stamp upon my back
cause I may be
the wrong gender colour or class

> *[Chorus]*

You can paint it which colour
you can divide it by class
you can say there is a weaker sex
and then stamp upon my back
but I don't care
because I have the means necessary

> *[Chorus]*

But don't you worry about me
and my sensibility
no don't you worry about me
and my sensibility
I will not take no time
to liberate our minds
no don't you worry about me
and my sensibility

> You can break the back but you can't break the
> spirit *[Repeat four times]*

© Random Order/SOCAN, 1993

Random **Order**

Toshi Reagon

Toshi Reagon is a savvy musician who fuses rock, funk and folk with gospel, migration blues and traditional music. Sweet and ethereal one moment, fierce and commanding the next, her vocals are mesmerizing, her sound seamless, her words empowering. She has shared stages with many artists and is a respected record producer with her own label, Pro-Momma LPs. Toshi's self-produced 1994 release, *The Rejected Stone*, drew upon the African-American song tradition revitalized by her mom, Bernice Johnson Reagon. In describing that album *Vibe Magazine* remarked, "Toshi is due for a shot in the rock Pantheon somewhere between Lenny Kravitz and the Indigo Girls." And the *New Yorker* wrote: "Reagon once gave up a major record deal because the suits wanted to reshape her image; now she releases her records herself. Her shows are celebrations — a shower of retro funk, urban blues and rock and they're all sung with evangelical fervour. To hear her is to believe." ◄

▶ OPENING NOTES

Date of birth
January 27, 1964

Place of birth
Atlanta, GA, USA

Astrological sign
Aquarius

Heritage
African-American

Siblings
One brother, two sisters

Language
English

Current residence
Brooklyn, NY, USA

Instruments
Vocals, bass, acoustic & electric guitar, drums

▶ ▶ ▶

Discography

- **Demonstrations**/T and R Tapes, Ladyslipper Distribution, 1986
- **Justice**/Flying Fish Records, 1990
- **The Rejected Stone**/Pro-Momma LPs, 1994
- **Kindness**/Folkways, 1997 release

A Capella

Listening to the Sounds of Everyday Life

I was born into a family at the centre of the non-violent civil rights movement of the 1960s. Both of my parents were a part of SNCC and were singers in the Original Freedom Singers. My brother, Kwan, and I were surrounded by their music. My mom and dad divorced when I was two, but we lived in Atlanta until I was seven, then moved with my mother to Washington, DC.

My mom, Bernice Johnson Reagon, was music director for the DC Black Repertory Company. My mom would take my brother and me to rehearsals, and the company gave me much of my early musical training. To this day, I still use some of the songs and information my young ears picked up hearing those talented people. Two years after moving to DC, my mom founded the group Sweet Honey In The Rock, and they were a big influence on me as well.

> "I appreciate and love music from all over the world."

Music was always important to me and I gravitated to a wide range of sounds. For example, when I was four, my mom bought me my first Jimi Hendrix album. I loved it, but I could also dig Pete Seeger. (In fact, I was named after Pete Seeger's wife, Toshi, who is also my Godmother. She ran the Clearwater Hudson Revival Festival for years and just recently retired.) Music, however, was not my first idea of a career. Sports were "it" for me when I was growing up. When I was fourteen, a leg injury put an end to the big-time sports career, and that's when I knew I wanted to be a professional musician with a band, making records and selling out concert halls. I taught myself bass, drums and guitar, and started writing songs and forming bands. When I was seventeen, I began playing with

Toshi **Reagon**

some women musicians just for fun, and that opened me up to a wider audience. I had already been working at Roadwork Productions, who booked Sweet Honey In The Rock and, at one time or another, had booked every major act in "women's music."

What is "women's music"? It's a powerful network of women artists, promoters, distributors, record companies, festivals and technicians who opened up the mainstream music industry to the idea that women are serious people in the business. There is not such a great necessity to use the label "women's music" anymore. But at one time it was an artistic and political necessary.

I started performing at the end of that era of "women's music." I played at women's music festivals and many of the great folk festivals, like Winnipeg Folk Festival and Clearwater

Fan Fare

Publicity
Music for Your Life
Productions, 328 Flatbush
Ave., Suite 124, Brooklyn,
NY, USA, 11238;
(718) 398-1187

Hudson Revival Festival. I also toured as a bass player for the reggae group Casselberry-Duprée, and, in 1990, I opened for the Lenny Kravitz "Let Love Rule" world tour. In 1991, I signed with Elektra Records; that deal didn't work out, but I came away from it with some serious production skills. I subsequently produced two Sweet Honey In The Rock records, and, in 1994, I produced and released my own album *The Rejected Stone* on my own label, Pro-Momma LPs.

Now, in 1996, I'm recuperating from my sixth hip surgery, writing a mystery novel and awaiting the release of my fourth album, *Kindness*. That album is acoustic, but my next CD, which I am just finishing, will feature my band. I'm also working on a recording project with my mom and brother, and I'm the music director with the dance group Urban Bush Women — recently, I composed an evening-length work for them called "Bones and Ashe," which was based on *The Gilda Stories* by Jewelle Gomez. The other thing I do is play bass for the reggae band Juca.

I would give any aspiring musician the same advice that my mom gave me when I was a kid and announced that I wanted to be musician. She told me stay off drugs and learn how to produce my own concerts. Today, I believe that every skill you can learn about this business is an asset, and, as a result, I produce concerts for myself and many of my friends. I still produce Sweet Honey In The Rock's anniversary concert every fall in Washington, DC.

People have described my music as so many things: rock, blues, folk, soft rock and so on, but I find pleasure in mixing it all up, using the ultra-rich African-American musical structures as my base. After that, anything goes — I appreciate and love music from all over the world and I also listen closely to the sounds of everyday life. I find music in almost all activities. Then I compose and play it because it is a way for me to be where I am. Through music, I can capture and transmit yesterday, and document and release today, so that they are available tomorrow. ◀

Toshi **Reagon**

This Could Be Heaven

Toshi Reagon

Consider this a wandering, a play on a thought.
Don't cast your eyes down or turn your ears off.
This is simple, but it's sure not easy.
Just another looking for a reason.

If this land is sacred I've been taking it for granted.
I'm relaxed in my ritual and my spiritual.
But with some imagination, I can see how it could
    be, how it should be, how it could be.

Chorus:
When I know that I've gone too far and I can just
    stand it.
I gotta wonder who I am and what's my hand in
    this.

Looking to a holy land, a place you believe might
    leave you void of your responsibilities.
Look at this holy land lying open, and now we have
    to think.
What have we done to this place?

Chorus:
When I know that I've gone too far and I can just
    stand it.
I gotta wonder who I am and what's my hand
    in this.
Looking to a magic place so far away.
Don't want to own the things around you don't
    wanna be caught with.
This could be heaven. *[repeat line four times]*

Bridge:
We can trust the rain to fall
    the wind to blow
    the flowers to grow
    the sun to shine
    the day to night
    humans to fight …

You never know for sure, so I show some respect.
If I get the 20/20, don't want to needs to regret.
Anything I've done while I'm here.

Chorus:
When I know that I've gone too far and I can
    and I can just stand it.
I gotta wonder who I am and what's my hand in
    this.
Looking to a magic place so far away.
Open your eyes today.
This could be heaven. *[repeat line four times]*

Bridge:
We can trust the rain to fall
    the spider to crawl
But can we trust the know-it-alls?
We can trust the rain to fall
    the wind to flow
    the flowers to grow
    the sun to shine
    the day to night
    the humans to fight
    this could be heaven …

Small
Judy

Judy Small is an Australian singer-songwriter who performs her songs of conscience, fun and passion all around the world. A memorable and moving performer, Judy spices her concerts with wit, humour, anger and compassion. Although her musical roots are in the folk tradition, she continually extends her boundaries, using blues, jazz, country, rock and even a taste of the classics, to bring her own distinctive style to the music she performs. As one critic has said: "Go and see Judy Small and have your ears blessed!" ◄

► OPENING NOTES

Date of birth
March 26, 1953

Place of birth
Coffs Harbour, New South Wales, Australia

Astrological sign
Aries

Heritage
Australian/British

Siblings
One brother, one sister

Languages
English, some French

Current residence
Melbourne, Victoria, Australia

Instruments
Vocals, guitar

► ► ►

Discography

- **A Natural Selection**/Good Things Enterprises (Australia), 1982
- **Ladies and Gems**/Plaza Records (Australia), 1984
- **Mothers, Daughters, Wives**/Redwood Records (USA), 1984
- **One Voice in the Crowd**/Crafty Maid Records (Australia), 1985; Redwood Records, 1985
- **Home Front**/Crafty Maid Records, 1988; Redwood Records , 1988
- **Snapshot**/Crafty Maid Records, 1990; Redwood Records , 1990
- **Second Wind**/Crafty Maid Records, 1993
- **Global Village**/Crafty Maid Records, 1995

Creating Moments of Hope

My musical roots are planted in the traditional music of the British Isles, English-speaking North America and Australia. Add to that a touch of the English music hall, and a smidgen of classical and country, and that's my style! I learned to sing in church and in school choirs, although, for as long as I can remember, I have sung for my own pleasure. Seven years of formal speech and drama lessons during my adolescence helped my voice enormously. I began writing little songs at the age of three or four, and did that in a more structured way from the age of fourteen. I learned to play guitar after my high-school music teacher (now a dear friend) decided that she would have a folk group at school, but if boys wanted to join, they would have to sing, and if girls wanted to join, they would have to play an instrument. I saved up for nine months, bought my guitar, was given a lesson on how to read a chord chart, and that was that. I taught myself after that first lesson, and I still cannot read or write music — so I always say I am a singer and songwriter, not a musician.

When I was growing up, my musical heroes were the musicians of the 1960s: Joan Baez, Mary Travers, Judith Durham, Janis Ian, Janis Joplin, Kathleen Ferrier and Jacqueline du Pres (the latter two were classical musicians, a contralto and a

> "If girls wanted to join, they would have to play an instrument."

cellist, respectively, and I loved both of them). I was strongly influenced by feminist and/or lesbians singers in the 1970s and 1980s, and today I am inspired by good music of any kind: I love Cecilia Bartoli, Joan Armatrading (she was in Melbourne just recently — what a concert!), the Tallis Scholars, Tina Arena (a young Australian pop singer — remember that name!), the orchestral music of

Judy Small

Vaughn Williams, and the choral music of Benjamin Britten, to name but a few. A very catholic collection!

I had my first gig as a folksinger when I was fifteen, at a restaurant outside my home town. It was cool! I was in a trio called the Three Pennies with two other girls from my school, and we sang together on and off for about two years. Other than that first performance, one of my most memorable gigs was a concert here in Melbourne in 1993 to launch my *Second Wind* album. That whole night was just perfect: there was a full house, a great audience, and my voice was working really well. Other performances I'll never forget: my first major concert as a solo performer, in the Sydney Town Hall in February 1982; touring Australia for the first time as a support act to the acoustic political-music band Redgum in 1983; singing the song "Mothers, Daughters, Wives" with Ronnie Gilbert at the Redwood Festival in Berkeley in September 1986; playing at the final concert of the *T inder* Festival in Denmark with Pete Seeger and Arlo Guthrie in August 1990; playing to 3,000 lesbians dressed to the nines in the concert hall of the Sydney Opera House for the 1991 Lesbian Festival; and playing at the Fourth United Nations Women's Non-Governmental Organization Forum in Beijing in 1995. All of these were

· · · · · · · · · · · ·

"My lesbianism is a central part of my identity as a musician."

· · · · · · · · · · · ·

memorable experiences — and there are probably a hundred more just like them. I've also played at a number of lesbian music festivals: Michigan; the U.S. National Women's Music Festival; the West Coast Women's Music and Comedy Festival; and the Pacific Northwest Women's Music and Cultural Jamboree in 1994. I also played at the Sydney Gay and Lesbian Mardi Gras Fair Day in 1995. I really have been incredibly fortunate!

I knew I was a lesbian when I was ten years old, though I could not have put that knowledge into words at the time. I did put it into words, at least for myself, at fourteen, but then I spent the next eight years desperately trying to prove that it wasn't so. I came out at twenty-two — that was more than twenty years ago, and I've never regretted it, nor wished my sexual orientation were otherwise. Certainly my lesbianism is a central part of my identity as a musician and I think my audiences all over the world know that I'm a lesbian — I make no bones about it — but I don't think I have an image as a "singer for lesbians" and I certainly don't see myself like that. I am a lesbian feminist folksinger whose music is for anyone who cares to listen.

These days, I am playing in a trio called Three Sheilas ("Sheila" is Australian slang for "broad" or "dame"), which is enormous fun. The other members are Kavisha Mazzella and Bronwyn Calcutt, and we sing original songs and some traditional music with a focus on celebrating women's experience. We are hoping to record a CD and

Judy **Small**

tour around Australia this year, but that depends on funding. My musical projects apart from the Three Sheilas are fairly ordinary because at the end of 1996 I'm intending to retire from the road and go back to being a lawyer for a living. Of course, that doesn't mean I won't sing; I'll sing for fun and pleasure. In the meantime, my partner, Sue, and I run our company from a bungalow in our backyard. Sue has three children: two sons, aged twenty-five and twenty-four, and a daughter, aged twenty. They're pretty well independent at this stage of their lives. Sue's family of origin live mostly in Melbourne, as do the children's father and paternal grandmother, so my day-to-day family life is centred in Melbourne.

Manager/agent
Sue Dyson, Crafty Maid Music, P.O. Box 304, Fairfield, Victoria, 3078, Australia; (61-3) 9481-7009 (phone); (61-3) 9482-5566 (fax); sdyson@netspace.net.au (e-mail)

Website
http://server.netspace. net.au/~sdyson/

What makes me play music? That's like asking what makes me breathe! I cannot imagine not playing music! However, I *do* think there is something that makes me want to play for a living — it's a combination of ego, politics (feminist and otherwise), the love of travel, and a desire to keep folk music alive. What I'm trying to convey to my audience is simple: Every human being has intrinsic worth in the world, and everyone needs to laugh, to grieve, to think, to be angry, to love and be loved and to live free. I want to convey that in as entertaining a way as possible.

My advice to aspiring lesbian musicians is as follows:

1. Never deny who you are, but recognize that, despite the rise of lesbian chic (which seemed to pass by me entirely!), we still live in a patriarchy, and if things are to change, all women need our support.

2. Figure out where you want to be: do you want to go for the fame, the glory, the big bucks? Then accept that the chances are extremely slight that you'll make it, and, if you do, you'll probably lose control of your music, and your career

"Do it your way, sister!"

will be short-lived. But I hear the rush is amazing! If you want to be around for longer, keep control of what you do, and realize that there is a living to be made out there — not a huge, fast living, but a very satisfying one.

3. Never sign any contract without talking to an independent lawyer (independent of the other party, that is).

4. Connect with your audience and give the audience the best that's in you at any given time — they deserve it, every time.

5. Have fun! If you don't enjoy it, don't do it.

6. Take no notice of older lesbian performers who think they know it all. Do it your way, sister! ◄

Judy **Small**

Hot Pick

No Tears for the Widow

Lyrics: Judy Small
Music: Judy Small and Robyn Payne

I never saw my mother cry until the night my father died
Married nearly thirty years, his dying had been hard
I remember how the family came to share the grief, the tears, the pain
And how her friends all gathered round and all the black-rimmed cards

The funeral was a large affair, the civic fathers all were there
Mother held up stoically she never shed a tear
But everyone there understood that she had entered widowhood
And life would never be the same, her status now was clear

Chorus:
And there were tears for the widow, tears for the widow
For the woman who had lost her love and must carry on alone
And Mother now writes "widow" in the space on all the forms
It's part of her identity like her grey hair or her name

My friend Amelia lost her love to cancer's slow and painful glove
The dying was no easier than my father's was back then
No black-rimmed cards came to her door, her grief and anguish all ignored
Except of course by closest friends who tried to understand

Her lover was described by all as a single woman living well
A tragic loss for family taken well before her time
When Amy left the funeral home she travelled to their house alone
Sat among familiar things and wept into the night

Chorus:
And there were no tears for the widow, no tears for the widow
For the woman who had lost her love and must carry on alone
And Amy still writes "single" in the space on all the forms
But she rages at the lie it tells and the loss that it ignores

And who can tell how many women live their lives in shadows
Unrecognized, unsympathized, unseen and disallowed
Who've lost not only lovers but often hearth and home
For marriage is a special word and only meant for some

Chorus:
And there were no tears for the widows, no tears for the widows
For the women who had lost lovers and must carry on alone
And life goes on but for them there is no space on any form
Yes marriage is a special word and only meant for some

© Crafty Maid Music, 1990

Judy **Small**

Topp Twins

The Topp Twins (Lynda and Jools) have been left-of-centre cultural icons in their home country of New Zealand for more than a decade. Voted New Zealand's "Entertainers of the Year" in 1987, they are well known for their distinctive Topp Twin yodel as well as their zany dyke comedy, and have performed extensively at women's festivals across the United States and in England, Australia and New Zealand. Most recently, they've launched their own comedy TV series and will soon be recording the songs from the show. ◄

▶ **OPENING NOTES**

Date of birth
May 14, 1958

Place of birth
Huntly, the Waikato,
New Zealand

Astrological sign
Taurus

Heritage
Scottish, English

Siblings
One brother

Languages
English, some Maori

Current residence
Auckland, New Zealand

Instruments
Vocals, guitar, banjo, mouth
harp, spoons, yodelling

▶ ▶ ▶

Left: Lynda
Right: Jools

The Radical Politics of Laughter

We grew up on a farm and were expected to just pitch in and do whatever had to be done, like everyone else — there were no fixed gender stereotypes. Our parents always encouraged us to be strong and independent. From an early age, we created our own entertainment, and music was a natural part of our environment. There was always live music at parties in the district or at home, and we also listened to old 78s of yodelling greats: Shirley Thomas, Judy Holmes (both Austalian) and our inspiration, Patsy Montana (from the United States, and the first woman to sell a million records). The neighbours who lived up the road from us — about twenty-five minutes on horseback — had an old wind-up gramophone, and Lynda used to listen to their yodel records, jump on her horse, race home, get the guitar out and try desperately to remember what she had heard. It took about three years, but from listening to these recordings and practising for

. . . .

"We always knew that we were lesbians."

. . . .

. . . .

Discography

- **Topp Twins Go Vinyl**/Topp Twins/independent, 1982
- **Twinset and Pearls**/Topp Twins/independent, 1984
- **No War in my Heart**/Topp Twins/independent, 1987
- **Wear Something Sexy**/Topp Twins/independent, 1991
- **Hightime**/Topp Twins/independent, 1992
- **Two Timing**/Topp Twins/independent, 1994

. . . .

Topp **Twins**

hours in the far paddock, we developed the distinctive Topp Twins yodel.

We made our debut performance at five years of age, singing "Walking in the Sunshine" with boaters and canes at a cousin's twenty-first birthday. When we were eleven, our brother gave us a guitar, and by the time we were in our early twenties, we had started playing "professionally." In the early 1980s, we began writing theatre shows, which include original songs, characters and comedy, and this has become a big part of what we do.

We always knew that we were lesbians, we just didn't know that what we were had a name until we saw some lesbians when we were sixteen, and we thought, "Hey, they're like us!" We both came out as lesbians when we were eighteen, and when we began to be known as performers a year or two later, the fact that we were gay hit all the main New Zealand newspapers. So, yes, we definitely have "lesbian" identities and, over the years, we have performed at most women's music festivals in the United States, and many lesbian-only

. . . .

"Practising for hours in the far paddock . . ."

. . . .

events in Australia, England and New Zealand. We are raging lesbians who sing country-and-western and political songs, yodel and perform theatre. The diversity of our performances and our audiences keeps us alive and keeps us going.

Recently, we just completed work on our own comedy TV series, which required us to create original music, and soon we'll be recording a new CD with songs from the series. In our spare time, Jools goes horse-riding; drives her old Bedford truck; walks her dog, Phantom; and hangs out with her girlfriend on the wild west coast, where they live most of the time. Lynda works at fixing up her Romany gypsy caravan; feeds the chooks; looks after her friend's three-year-old son, Arlo; cooks; does theatre production; and spends non-working time with her girlfriend.

Our musical philosophy can be summed up like this: We play music because we love to — it's who we are and what we do. But it's also more than just music — it's about really giving people a great show, touching their lives, making them laugh. All sorts of people come to our shows — grandmothers, farmers, kids, gays, lesbians — so to get all of them laughing at the same time is a radical thing. It breaks down barriers. We believe in giving everything we can to our audience, which is why we've always been out, even way back before it was "chic." We felt we couldn't hold back who we were; otherwise, our performance would suffer.

Our advice to aspiring lesbian musicians is: Be who you are, find your own voice, be prepared to work at all aspects of the business, stay in control — and have lots of fun. ◄

Fan Fare

Management/ fan club
Arani Cuthbert, Topp Twins Management, P.O. Box 5986, Wellesley St., Auckland, New Zealand; (64-9) 3765-239 (phone); (64-9) 3765-279 (fax)

107

Topp **Twins**

Martina

Topp Twins

Chorus:
I'm leaving tonight with a heartful of sorrow
I should have loved you more, not let you walk out the door
And never let you go.

Oh Oh Martina I hate how we fought
It's only a game now the ball's in your court
Love one

    [Chorus]

Oh Oh my darling I loved you each day
You took me in your arms moved me with your charms
Now you'll have to pay
One million dollars

    [Chorus]

Oh Oh Martina I'm setting you free
I don't miss the sex I'm going out with your ex
She's going to write a book about me

    [Chorus]

Tribe 8

Voted one of *Rolling Stone*'s "Twelve Artists on the Edge" in 1995, Tribe 8 (the name comes from the word "tribadism," meaning, in Tribe's own words, "humpin' on chicks") are "San Francisco's own all-dyke, all-out, in-your-face, blade-brandishing, gang-castrating, dildo-swingin', bullshit-detecting, aurally pornographic, Tribe Neanderthal-pervert band of patriarchy-smashing snatchlickers." Feminist and "prosex," the Tribe (Slade, Breedlove, Mah, Tantrum and Flipper) are on a musical mission to annihilate repression of any kind — including the repression that comes from their own kind. As artists, Tribe 8 have their serious side, dealing with topics like self-destructive drug abuse and national politics, but they thrive on comic relief. ◄

► OPENING NOTES

Posing as a punk-rock band, the five above-named fugitives have been gathering, plotting and planning for the last five years, after having met in prison and at twelve-step meetings. They have toured Europe twice and the United States five times. Amerikkkan gigs have included the Michigan Womyn's Music Festival, where they met Alix Dobkin and united old-school Birkenstock feminists with new-school punk-rock babes, causing 8,000 naked women to riot. They are featured in the soon-to-be-released feature-length film, *A Gun for Jennifer*, about a gang of vigilante go-go dancers. Improvised musically with Kathy Acker on material produced by Hal Wilner. Had starring role in the Bloomington, IN, mayoral race of 1995 as notorious and nefarious youth corruptors. Also caused a political stir — and our founding fathers to spin their graves — when they played Provincetown's Town Hall. Have barely survived malnutrition, insanity and jealous lovers while trying to stay drug/alcohol-free, vegetarian and out of trouble on the road. Warning! These five fugitives should be considered extremely dangerous. They are a threat to our nation's security and morals, and to the future of the family. ► ► ►

A Capella

Getting Live Nude Girls for Free

Breedlove

Spent college days organizing dyke militia that raided frat parties, saving rape victims. Ran amok with uzis at one particularly ugly party, revived girls with homemade speed and finished off kegs while frats writhed in own blood. Indicted for attempted murder with the intent to maim. Spent fifteen years at Atascadero, California's prison for the criminally insane. Released on good behaviour, on condition that she go to drug rehab.

Favourite Slogan: "Kill 'em all, let gawd sort 'em out."

Interests: Sex, revolution, chain-saws, inciting riot with written and spoken word.

Business: Lickety Split All-Girl Bike Messenger Delivery

Favourite Hangout: Red Dora's, The Bearded Lady Dyke Cafe

• •

Discography

- **Pig Bitch** (7")/Harp Records, 1992
- **There's a Dyke in the Pit** (7", EP)/Outpunk, 1992
- **Bitches in Brew** (7")/Lickout, 1993
- **Speed Fortress** (compilation CD)/Kill Rock Stars, 1993
- **By the Time We Get to Colorado** (12", EP)/Outpunk, 1993
- **Oversize Ego** (compilation CD)/Outpunk, 1994
- **Allen's Mom** (7")/Outpunk, 1994
- **Fist City**/Alternative Tentacles Records, 1995
- **Roadkill Cafe** (7")/Alternative Tentacles Records, 1996
- **Snarkism**/Alternative Tentacles Records, 1996

• •

Clockwise from left: Mah, Flipper, Breedlove, Slade, Tantrum

"Tribe 8 . . . meaning 'humpin' on chicks'."

Mah

Ran a brothel in Boulder, CO. Feds cancelled indictment when she revealed photos of federal agents in compromising positions. In exchange for dropped charges, agreed to close brothel and get out of the business. Invested savings in tattoos and music equipment.

Former/Current Bands: Bass player for ASF (Anti-Scrunti Faction), Slow Club

Interests: Chix, tattoos

Favourite Hangout: Black and Blue Tattoo Parlor

Slade Bellum
Drums

Lynn Breedlove
Vocals

Lynn Flipper
Guitar

Leslie Mah
Guitar

Tantrum
Bass

Tantrum

Top assassin for West Indian Mafia. Computer hack. Indicted for espionage and embezzlement after cracking top secret CIA computer files and diverting funds from Pentagon and Chevron bank accounts to her homeland. Wanted by Interpol on three continents.

Former Bands: Random Order, 7 Cent Posse

Interests: Babes

Favourite Hangout: Tour van

Slade

Bomb expert responsible for thirteen Walmart bombings in the early 1980s. Never caught.

Former Bands: Industrial Rainforest, Burning Witches

Interests: Girls

Favourite Hangouts: Used-car lots, abandoned warehouses

Flipper

Robbed sixteen banks before the age of eighteen. Tried as a minor and released after five years. In her defence, stated, "At first I just did it to impress girls, but then I realized it was pretty fun."

Former Bands: Air guitar for Led Zeppelin & Jimi Hendrix

Interests: Chickeebabes, coffee

Business: Red Dora's, The Bearded Lady Dyke Cafe, where the motto is: "Whatever the ladies want, that's what we're here for."

Favourite Hangouts: Street corners, crap games ◄

Fan Fare

Management
Girlie Action, 270 Lafayette Street, Suite 907, New York, NY, USA, 10012; (212) 334-3200 (phone); (212) 334-4413 (fax)

Website
http://www.jett.com/tribe8/tribe8.html

Wrong Bathroom

Lyrix: Tantrum, Flipper, Breedlove, Mah
Music: Tribe 8

Punk rock band touring the USA
Stopping along the Amerikkkan highway
Pull into the truckstop cuz I gotta take a leak
Everybody staring like I'm some kinda freak
Fuck all this attention, I think I'll try to sneak
Into the ladies' room without getting caught
What? I just gotta use the pot
I gotta show you what I got?

"Excuse me, sir? Over by the stall.
Wrong bathroom. The men's room's down the hall."

So I pull up my shirt to show I'm the right gender
But the looks you're giving me are anything but tender
What's your problem? I ain't got a member
Fine, I'll go into the boy's room
But it really fucking stinks
What's with your aim boy? You trying to hit the
    tank?
Your tomcat spray ferments so rank
So for you a little present
bloody tampon on the sink

Yeah my hair's pink I'm the missing link
You don't have a missing link bathroom

"Is that a he or a she?
Is that a him or a her?
Oh excuse me, ma'am ... uh, sir?"
Am I supposed to feel ashamed
Cuz you're confused
Cuz I don't fit into your box
You loser

"Excuse me ma'am your titties are kinda small
I'm still confused ..."

Poor tired pathetic little sheep
Trying to limit me
With your dyke-otomies
Simple minds know two kinds
And I'm number three
You and Rush don't know shit about me
So let me pee
And gimme my free
Condiments in every bathroom.

© Alternative Tentacles Records, 1996

Left to right: Miss Jones, Alics, Lucy, Angie, Sam

CHARLOTTE BRENNAN

The Well Oiled Sisters

The Well Oiled Sisters are Scottish "Hooligan hillbilly honeys, putting the cow grrl back into country." Brewed in Scotland and distilled in London, England, the Sisters are: Lucy, the original Dirty Cowgirl; Alics, plays like a devil, sings like an angel; Sam, blonde, beautiful, with biceps to die for; Miss Jones, mad, bad and dangerous to know; and Angie Dypso, a recreational dypsomaniac with a deep throaty voice. Together, they play cowpunk country that's fast, furious, lusty, gutsy and full of tongue-in-cheek irreverence. ◄

making music

Alics
Bass, back-up vocals

Angie Dypso
Accordion, back-up vocals, guitar, percussion

Lucy
Lead vocals, guitar

Miss Jones
Fiddle

Sam
Drums

► OPENING NOTES
(for the group)

Place of birth
Edinburgh and Glasgow, Scotland

Heritage
Scottish

Language
English

Current residence
London, U.K.

116

Cunnilingual Cowgrrrls

We are cunnilingual, and speak Scottish and English fluently. The band consists of: one Gemini, one Capricorn, one Aquarius, one Aries, one Librarian and one Zebra. Raised in the purple-headed Mary Hills, we have been known to bathe in woad and, despite being based in London, England, we are still frighteningly Scottish.

Our musical roots are diverse, and include the Celtic, punk, country and rockabilly traditions, as well as light operetta. Our musical influences are varied and mostly dead! They include Hank Williams, the Partridge Family, Elvis, Tammy Wynette, the Nolan Sisters, Gwar, Rolf Harris, Discharge, Deanna Durbin (and the sound of a cork being softly rubbed against a bottle). We all learned to play music as a matter of survival in our childhood years

. . . .

"We're trying to promote fun, freedom, assertiveness, drunkenness, excess and underwire bras."

. . . .

in Scotland; the only other professions open to us were "town drunk" and "coal miner." Our first "professional" gig (Edinburgh '92) paid in tequila. Our most memorable gigs include playing Estonia in the Baltic States; Pimba (population thirty-six) in the Australian outback; Zenith Stadium, Paris (supporting Morrissey); Caceres, Spain (in front of 25,000 people); and the "Broken Arms," Bradford. Our lesbian gigs have taken place on the main stage at Europride, the women's tent at

. . . .

Discography

- **Alcohol and Tears**/Cycle Records, 1994

. . . .

London Pride (several times) and the Amsterdam Women's Festival. All our gigs have a large following of women, and we are known as a dyke band by our dyke fans, but we hope to appeal to everyone.

. . . .

"The only other professions open to us were town drunk and coal miner."

. . . .

We intend to record a second CD this year, and have firm plans to play Europe, the United States, Canada, anywhere and everywhere. Past musical collaborations include Morrissey, the Village People and Archie Roach & Ruby Hunter (Australia). Also, Joe Strummer from the Clash, who discovered us busking in London and gave us our first gig.

When we're onstage, we consider ourselves to be musicians first and foremost. Our sexuality, though not irrelevant, is not the most important thing about us — and, in fact, one member of the Sisters is straight. Like most lesbians, we have all had different sexual experiences and identities at one time or another. Our present sexual proclivities are just one facet of what we write and perform about. We consider religion, politics, love, fun and sex to be equally valid subjects, and they, along with our sexuality, make up the overall identity of The Well Oiled Sisters. Basically, all human experience is important to us. Our songs are gender specific — we don't sing about loving boys or men and we are proud of what and who we are. We also feel

Fan Fare

Management
Pat Gibbons,
Well Oiled Sisters,
61 Thornhill Houses,
Thornhill Road, Islington,
London, N1 1PB, U.K.;
(0181) 986-2551 (phone);
(0181) 483-1743 (fax)

Distribution
Direct Distribution, U.K.

E-mail fan clan
bdypso@dircon.co.uk

that our sexuality has allowed us freedom from the constraints and restrictions of a conventional heterosexual lifestyle, and we celebrate and indulge in this liberty to the fullest.

. . . .

"Be out if you wish, but don't be stereotyped and bound by your sexuality."

. . . .

In summary, we enjoy playing music because we adore showing off and getting free beer and a shag after every gig! We're trying to promote fun, freedom, assertiveness, drunkenness, excess and underwire bras. Our advice to lesbian musicians is: Be out if you wish, but don't be stereotyped and bound by your sexuality. Also, don't get boys to play bass and drums — it's a cop-out. Girls are perfectly capable of playing rhythm! And: Get your head down and practise! ◄

It Ain't Hard Being Easy

Edwards/Gate-Eastley

One more drink and yes I will kindly leave
I'll take my custom someplace else
I know my legs will end up behind my neck
Wreak some havoc and paint this whole town red

> *Chorus:*
> It ain't hard being easy
> Not for a hungry girl like me
> It ain't hard being easy
> And I don't care

Hit the bars I lost my balance hit the floor
I bounced back up when someone caught my eye
She smiled at me I swear she did I know she did
Got booze on my breath and one thing on my mind

> *[Chorus]*

All I want is a wet warm place to park my face
Fill me up and take me for a ride
I'm a disgrace but I like what lies
in your ice blue eyes
So take me home do exactly as you please

> *[Chorus]*

© Edwards/Gate-Eastley, 1994

Cris Williamson & Tret Fure

C ris Williamson is an acclaimed pioneer of women's music, a spirit healer and a teacher of the "art of the possible." Tret Fure's talents as a musician are matched only by her ease behind the recording console, where she has engineered and produced a number of albums. Together, Cris and Tret have been making memorable music for some fifteen years, and their diversity of skills has led them to the natural next step: They recently announced plans to launch their own music label, Wolf Moon Records. ◄

▶ OPENING NOTES
(Cris Williamson)

Date of birth
February 15, 1947

Place of birth
Deadwood, SD, USA

Astrological sign
Aquarius

Heritage
English, Irish, Scottish, unkown

Siblings
One sister, one brother

Languages
English, a bit of Spanish

Current residence
Marcola, OR, USA

Instruments
Vocals, piano, guitar

▶ ▶ ▶

▶ OPENING NOTES
(Tret Fure)

Date of birth
March 18, 1951

Place of birth
Schaller, IA, USA

Astrological sign
Pisces

Heritage
Italian, Norwegian

Siblings
Three brothers

Languages
English, some French, currently learning Italian

Current residence
Marcola, OR, USA

Instruments
Vocals, guitar, keyboards, harmonica, banjo

▶ ▶ ▶

A Capella

Long Time Becoming

Cris

I've been playing music for forty-three years, professionally for thirty-three years. My roots are in folk, rock and classical music. I took piano lessons from Grades One to Seven, and vocal lessons all through high school and into college. I am self-taught on guitar. My first album was released on Avanti Records when I was sixteen. Before that, I had been performing forever — with choirs and ensembles, and in talent shows.

When I was young, I was influenced by a lot of women: my mother, my teachers, women who ran ranches and managed

. . . .

Discography [Cris Williamson)]

- **Artistry of Cris Williamson**/Avanti, 1964
- **A Step at a Time**/Avanti, 1965
- **The World Around Cris Williamson**/Avanti, 1965
- **Cris Williamson**/Ampex, 1971 (reissued by Olivia, 1981)
- **Cris Williamson** (EP)/Kickback, 1972
- **The Changer and the Changed**/Olivia, 1974
- **Live Dream**/Olivia, 1978
- **Strange Paradise**/Olivia, 1978
- **Lumiere**/Pacific Cascades, 1982
- **Blue Rider**/Olivia, 1982
- **Meg & Cris at Carnegie Hall**/Olivia, 1983
- **Portrait**/Olivia, 1983
- **Prairie Fire**/Olivia, 1984
- **Snow Angel**/Olivia, 1985
- **Wolf Moon**/Olivia, 1987
- **Country Blessed** (with Teresa Trull)/Second Wave/Olivia, 1989
- **The Best of Cris Williamson**/Olivia, 1990
- **Circle of Friends**/Olivia, 1991
- **Postcards from Paradise** (with Tret Fure)/Olivia, 1993

. . . .

Left: Cris
Right: Tret

Cris **Williamson** & Tret **Fure**

families, and women who were fire guards, by themselves all summer long. Growing up on the prairies beside the Rocky Mountains, and in my particular family, was a special experience. There was no running water or electricity in our home in the early years. Neighbours lived at a great distance. I belonged

"I had time to dream and imagine."

to my family and yet to myself — I had time to dream and imagine.

One of my main musical influences was, and continues to be, Ella Fitzgerald. Besides Ella, I was inspired when I was younger by Chopin, Dylan, Judy Collins, Joan Baez, Joni Mitchell, Janis Joplin, Gershwin, Edith Piaf and the Beatles (just to name a few). Today I'm inspired by Ella, Joni, Sting, James Taylor, Peter Gabriel, Shawn Colvin, Paul Brady, Jane Siberry, Ferron, Ani DiFranco and the Band. There are many, many great artists out there now. ◄

Tret

My roots are also in folk music. I've been playing music for forty-one years, professionally for thirty years. I studied piano from ages five to seven, and, when I was six, I was writing songs and playing them for my teacher's high-school students. We left Iowa when I was seven, and my parents sold my piano. They failed to get another when we landed in Illinois, so I picked up the violin and played it from the fourth grade until high school. Then I left the violin for the guitar, which I taught myself to play. I've been playing guitar for thirty-five years.

My heritage is rich with Italian passion, food, humour, and the old bones of Norwegians and their love for the earth. My family travelled around this country [the United States] together in the car, so I got to see a great deal of landscape. My mother gave me cooking skills, my father gave me gardening skills and my brothers

"My heritage is rich with Italian passion, food, humour, and the old bones of Norwegians."

Discography [Tret Fure]

- **Mousetrap** (with Spencer Davis)/United Artists, 1970
- **Tret Fure**/MCA, 1973
- **Terminal Hold**/Second Wave, 1984
- **Edges of the Heart**/Second Wave, 1986
- **Time Turns the Moon**/Second Wave, 1990
- **Postcards from Paradise** (with Cris Williamson)/Olivia, 1993

taught me how to survive in a masculine world. My strongest female role models were my mother, my second-grade teacher and my senior English teacher.

When I was young, my musical inspiration came from Bob Dylan, Judy Collins, Joan Baez and Phil Ochs — I grew up listening to them; later, I listened to Joni Mitchell, James Taylor and the Beatles. Lowell George was a big influence on my music in the early to mid-1970s. Now my inspiration comes from artists like Joni, Sting, James Taylor, Peter Gabriel, Shawn Colvin, Paul Brady, Jane Siberry and Bonnie Raitt. ◄

Cris and Tret

For both of us, our coming-out experiences were more like "becoming experiences." The process of coming out was gradual in that we eventually chose to be with women more than with men. Now we are married for life to each other. We both feel that we have identities as "lesbian musicians" for three reasons: because of who we are; because of who our

"Our musical relationship continues to grow and unfold."

main audience is; and because the genre of women's music has, from the beginning, included so many lesbians.

A memorable musical highlight for both of us was the first Carnegie Hall concert with Meg Christian. Cris was a featured artist, and Tret was a band member, co-producer and engineer for the recording (*Meg & Cris at Carnegie Hall*). We did two back-to-back sold-out shows and it was magnificent — it was a first.

These days, we play with a band only when we record and for special events. Otherwise we *are* the band: Cris Williamson and Tret Fure. We are currently recording our second album as a duo, on our own label, Wolf Moon Records. The album is called *Between the Covers*. Writing together has been a

great development for both of us. We are collaborating with June Millington again on this project, and our musical relationship continues to grow and unfold. When you can read another musician's mind, you are a giant step ahead. In our spare time, which is rare, our activities include reading, movies and gardening. Tret loves to cook and is an amateur carpenter — she builds all the out-buildings on our place. We love to work on our place together ... making beauty.

Why do we want to play music? Because it's in us. It's like breathing. It's who we are. Our advice to aspiring musicians is this: Find ways to be yourself at all times in the world. Push forward, don't get discouraged. Make sure your life and your work are one. It's a tough life but a rewarding one. And always be mindful that you stand on the shoulders of giants. ◄

Fan Fare

Agent
Tam Martin, 25-6 NW 23rd Pl., #416, Portland, OR, USA, 97210-3534;
(503) 281-3874;
TamMartin@aol.com

Website
http://www.hypernet.com/cris&tret.html

Cris **Williamson** & Tret **Fure**

Hot Pick

Surrender Dorothy

Tret Fure and Cris Williamson

I've got so many hours,
so much time,
a heart full of romance
(And) you on my mind.
Lonely long distance,
wires in the wind
measure the miles
'til I see you again.

It's a long way to the Wizard,
(It's a) long way home,
(I'm) calling from Kansas.
can you hear the wind moan?
Weakened condition,
(From the) edge of my eye
saw the word "surrender"
written clear across the sky.

Chorus:
Surrender Dorothy,
time and again,
surrender …
the will, oh, the will
of the wind.
Surrender Dorothy,
time and again,
Surrender.

(There's a) tornado blowin',
Bending the plains,
My heart is twisting.
Will I see you again.
Oh, how it pushes me,
clear down to the bone
sing a song of bravery.
There's no place like Home.

[Chorus]

Click your heels three times and head for Home.
In your dreams, you find you're not alone.
There's no place like Home.

Sisters
Wyrd

The Wyrd Sisters (lesbians Nancy Reinhold and Kim Baryluk, and their straight sister Lianne Fournier) are not truly weird, although they might lay claim to descriptions such as "unusual," "unique," "original" and "provocative." The musical trio takes its name from the ancient Triple Goddess, who represents the circular nature of life and the phases of the moon.

As musicians, the Wyrd Sisters have shown that a strong background in songwriting and skill in vocal harmony is an inspiring combination. In a short time, they have matured from being a fledgling but promising trio in their native province of Manitoba, Canada, to an accomplished ensemble on the brink of national and international recognition. ◄

► OPENING NOTES
(Nancy Reinhold)

Date of birth
March 6, 1956

Place of birth
Buffalo, NY, USA

Astrological sign
Pisces

Heritage
Norwegian, German, British

Siblings
Three sisters

Language
English

Current residence
Winnipeg, MB, Canada

Instruments
Vocals, guitar

► OPENING NOTES
(Kim Baryluk)

Date of birth
April 21, 1959

Place of birth
Winnipeg, MB, Canada

Astrological sign
Taurus (on cusp of Aries)

Heritage
Primarily Ukranian

Siblings
Three sisters, one brother

Languages
English, a bit of Ukranian

Current residence
Winnipeg, MB, Canada

Instruments
Vocals, guitar, keyboards, harmonica, mandolin

Breaking Down Barriers

Nancy

I was always, always involved with music. When I was very young, I listened to my dad's classical record collection; my sister and I even had our own unique rendition of "The Nutcracker." My mother listened to Ella Fitzgerald and Billie Holiday, so I grew up hearing some jazz. And, of course, my older sister was cool, so whatever she liked I liked. Early on I listened mostly to Joni Mitchell, James Taylor, Crosby, Stills & Nash — and, yes, Peter, Paul & Mary. I knew every lyric and every harmony. I also sang in choirs and was in love with choral singing. Then, when I was in Grade Four, I got my

> "The band has had opportunities ... to share festival stages with some of our heroines."

first real guitar from Sears. I was thrilled! I took some lessons but was just too shy to carry it off, so I quit the formal training. I remained a closeted singer-songwriter and guitarist for years and ventured out only occasionally, though my mother often begged me to perform.

Finally, in my mid-twenties, I experienced a time of huge change. I came out about my lesbianism, after years of agonizing over it. My family was completely accepting and

Clockwise from left: Nancy, Lianne, Kim

Discography

- **Leave a Little Light**/independent release, 1993
- **New Canadian Women Singers** (compilation CD)/CBC, 1993
- **Inside the Dreaming**/independent release, 1995

somewhat relieved, I think, since they had been waiting patiently for me to bring up the subject. At the same time, Kim Baryluk and I started our first band, along with three other women. It didn't last long, but we had some good fun and

> ## "Those sweet moments when the barriers break down between you and the audience."

our first real taste of performing. Over the next several years I performed a few times — sometimes solo, sometimes with a friend — but it wasn't until the advent of the Wyrd Sisters in 1991 that I started to consider working at music professionally. The Wyrd Sisters have had a strong following from the beginning — especially, though not exclusively, in the women's community.

Since 1991, the band has had opportunities to work with some wonderful musicians and to share festival stages with some of our heroines and mentors, including Sweet Honey in the Rock, Ferron and Cris Williamson. One of our favourite spontaneous musical collaborations was with the Flirtations at the 1994 Winnipeg Folk Festival. We hastily learned a couple of each other's songs and then performed together at a workshop stage, to our own delight as well as that of the audience. We've also worked extensively with jazz pianist, composer and friend Marilyn Lerner, and have played folk festivals in Canada from Winnipeg to Vancouver to Inuvik. Our venues have included concert halls, bars, houses and marches. We have yet to play any lesbian festivals or women's festivals, but that will come, most likely as we venture more frequently into the United States.

The three original members of the band were all lesbians. In 1993, our soprano departed, and Kim and I began the search for her replacement. We hired Lianne Fournier, a Winnipeg jazz vocalist with a knack for the keyboard, to fill in while we auditioned potential Wyrdos.

In the end, Lianne worked out so well that she just stayed on. She's not a dyke (she's oxysexual, she says!) but we keep her around to provide a bit of balance!

We have found the music business to be a challenging, frustrating, extremely gratifying and absolutely insane way to make a living. But, there are still those sweet moments when the barriers break down between you and the audience, when the music somehow releases all of its strength or humour or anger or love, when the instruments hug the vocals and the lyrics tug the heart — and those sweet moments temper all of the insanity and frustration, and pull you along and hypnotize you. And you just can't resist.

Kim

As a child, my greatest exposure to music happened in church. My parents are both atheists, but in order to please my grandmother, we children were sent to the Ukrainian Catholic cathedral at the end of our block. The church had a magnificent choir that sang in rich and glorious harmony. This choir music gave me my musical roots. When I was a teenager, I received a guitar for my birthday and taught myself chords from the back page of a magazine. I'd write songs and poems and stories, mostly

- - - - - - - - - - - - - - - - -

"Being a musician usually means living in poverty."

- - - - - - - - - - - - - - - - -

for my own enjoyment. I always knew I would have a musical career one day, but I was in no rush. It was important for me to be financially secure, and I knew that being a musician usually means living in poverty, so working and making cold hard cash was my first priority.

When I was in my early thirties and felt financially stable, I formed the Wyrd Sisters with Nancy Reinhold and another woman. When the band first started up, the three of us all

played guitars, but since then I've picked up some keyboards, harmonica and mandolin. Since we're generally able to bring in other musicians to play with us, I play as little as possible these days. I prefer to be able to focus my energy on creating a strong performance.

We always assumed that, as lesbians who write feminist music, the Wyrd Sisters would be strictly a women's-music act. To our surprise, we garnered a mainstream and folk audience rather quickly. It's not unusual for us to play to totally straight audiences, though in places where we're better known there are always a good many dykes in the audience. I do identity as a lesbian musician, though, and am completely comfortable with that. Coming out was an easy, rather joyful experience for me. My family accepts me and my lifestyle as a matter of course. I was eighteen or nineteen when I came out, and have found and created a comfortable community for myself since then. I do not tolerate homophobia or "isms" of any sort, and I educate where I can and fight where I can't.

My advice to young lesbian performers is this: Have money. Performing is expensive. Recording, touring and marketing are expensive. Do not sign any record deals until you've come far enough yourself to call the shots. Market products to sell yourself — even tee-shirts and demo tapes. Products such as these bring in money. As well, you must know your audience and believe in yourself. I love people who believe in you and your music working for you as agents and managers. And, above all, live your dreams and have fun. ◀

Fan Fare

Management
Margo Charlton Creative Services, Canada; (204) 775-5320 (phone); (204) 775-3664 (fax); marym@ solutions.net (e-mail)

Agent
Paquin Entertainment, Canada;
(204) 697-0650 (phone); (204) 697-0903 (fax)

Publicity
Shelley Breslaw Publicity, Canada;
(204) 453-0015 (phone); (204) 284-1190 (fax)

Website
http://www.ivideo.mb.ca/ wyrd

Dance Little Brother

Kim Baryluk

Saw my Brother just the other day
He was pale and weak he was fading away
And though we sat and shot the shit we had nothing
   to say
What can you say?

What can you do in times like this
When a backward glance or a stolen kiss
Can make you Prince or Pauper
Make you hit or miss

If you only knew him when he used to dance
With his slicked-black hair and poured-on pants
He could really strut his stuff
And turn a head or two

   Chorus:
   Dance little brother like you used to do
   Dance little brother like you

When he was born he was the chosen one
The golden child the fair-haired son
He was the hopes and dreams of a future come at
   last
Grew up too fast

As his eyes dim so do ours
Years into days, days into hours
The hopes and dreams of a future flying past

We've got micro-discs and test-tube wombs
We've got nuclear bombs and men on the moon
But do we have a hope in hell of bringing that boy
   home?

   [Chorus]

© Kim Baryluk, 1993

Zrazy

In the last few years, the Irish band Zrazy (Carole Nelson and Maria Walsh) has been sweeping up awards in their native land and winning a devoted following abroad — all this while coming out to media and the public (even before k.d.!). In 1993, they won the "Best New Band Award" at the Irish National Music Critics Awards, and their first single, "I'm in Love with Mother Nature," became the highest new entry in the Irish pop charts. A year later, Zrazy was featured in every category of the reader's polls in *Hotpress Music Paper*'s "Top Ten" lists. (*Hotpress Music Paper* is the Irish equivalent of *Rolling Stone*). The band's current album, *Permanent Happiness*, contains a new gay anthem, "Come Out Everybody," that has been described as "a totally 1990s lazy political song." ◄

► OPENING NOTES
(Carole Nelson)

Place of birth
London, England

Astrological sign
Sagittarius

Heritage
English

Siblings
One sister, one brother

Languages
English, French

Current residence
Dublin, Ireland

Instruments
Vocals, keyboard, saxophone, tin whistle

► OPENING NOTES
(Maria Walsh)

Place of birth
Tipperary, Ireland

Astrological sign
Taurus

Heritage
Irish

Siblings
One brother

Languages
English, French, a little Spanish

Current residence
Dublin, Ireland

Instruments
Vocals, flute, bodhran, blues harmonica

Out in the Mainstream

Carole

I grew up hearing a mixture of classical, jazz and rock music. I first learned to play an instrument when I was ten and took piano lessons at school. My female role models when I was growing up were Joni Mitchell, Marie Curie and Gladys Aylward (a missionary — I was very young!). As a young musician, I was inspired by Joni Mitchell, David Bowie and Steely Dan. Today, I listen to Massive Attack, baroque and world music, and Hildegard Von Bingen. I've been playing music for thirty-three years now, and it is my life and soul. I know no other path.

My most memorable performance was playing solo sax in

Left: Maria
Right: Carole

Barcelona in 1980. One of Zrazy's most memorable performances was a collaboration with other musicians during an International Women's Day performance in Dublin in 1993. We were joined on stage by all the major female Irish artists — it was the best backing vocal line-up we are ever likely to experience.

These days Zrazy is touring our second album, *Permanent*

. . . .

"Music is my life and soul."

. . . .

Happiness. I have also been involved in a project with the lesbian playwright and author Emma Donoghue from Dublin — I composed songs and music for her play *Ladies and Gentlemen*. In what spare time I have,

. . . .

Discography

- **Give It All Up**/Vélo, 1993
- **Permanent Happiness**/Alfi, 1995
- **Sing, Don't Sign** (a benefit album for Idaho's Decline to Sign campaign)/Reprise, 1996

. . . .

I practise t'ai chi, watch films, go to soccer matches and enjoy my lesbian social life.

Why do I play music? Well, I came out when I was twenty years old, as a student at Cambridge University, and although the core of my musical being is not sexed, I do take a strong lesbian stance in the world. In 1980, I formed the personal ambition to be an out lesbian making records that would be heard in mainstream society. I achieved this ambition in 1993 when Zrazy became lesbian celebrities in the Irish media. The single *"I'm in Love with Mother Nature"* was like a battle cry to both the music industry and the public. Nowadays I'm interested in music as a healing force for myself, for the gay community and for the world at large.

My advice to aspiring lesbian musicians is: Follow the muse and be out and proud. ◄

Maria

I remember listening to Irish traditional music and blues on the radio, and I took piano lessons and learned to play other instruments through family friends. Today, I mostly play the flute and bodran (the traditional Irish drum). My female role model growing up was Billie Jean King. My musical idols were Mary Jordan (Irish traditional flute), Rory Gallagher (the great Irish blues and rock guitarist), Grace Jones with Sly and Robbie,

. . . .

"Living in the midst of nature inspires me."

. . . .

Dusty Springfield and Ella Fitzgerald. These days I'm inspired by different musical disciplines in general, and, in particular, by my own emotions. I want to translate those emotions into music that enters the soul. Living in Ireland and living in the midst of nature inspires me to do this. In my spare time, I like to have a glass of red wine in one hand and a book in the other. And I love walking by the sea, and dancing when I need a release.

My most memorable performance was at Zrazy's first gig —

we were still very much amateurs, but the audience loved us. Since then, there have been too many memorable gigs to mention them all (among them: International Women's Day in Dublin in 1994, Berlin in 1993, Texas, Toronto …). We have also had many great performances at lesbian music festivals: doing the day stage at Michigan in 1993 in scorching heat — great; playing under starry Texas skies at the Lone Star Women's festival — wonderful. However, even though I came out when I was twenty-two, and came out again in public with Zrazy in 1992, I don't feel as though I really have an identity as a lesbian musician. I find the label more and more limiting.

My advice to lesbians who want to be musicians is simple: Play everywhere. ◄

Fan Fare

Agent
Madeleine Seiler, Ireland;
353-1-497-6451 (phone);
353-1-497-6719 (fax)

Fan club
Zrazy, P.O. Box 103, Blackrock, County Dublin, Ireland

Website
http://www.iol.ie/~zrazy

E-mail
zrazy@iol.ie

Come Out Everybody

Lyrics: Carole Nelson and Kim Fowley
Music: Carole Nelson

Cruel worlds killed the children
And swallowed the best
We all grew up knowing
We could never rest
We were so rejected
We were despised
We learned to say nothing
We learned to tell lies

Then I turn on the radio
In the dark, in my bed and I'm all alone
And I hear someone
Saying our time has come
And I want to believe it step out into the sun
With my sisters and my brothers
It's time to have some fun

Come out everybody
Let the good times roll
Come out everybody
Its time to take control
Come out everybody
Listen to your soul
Come out everybody
Let the good times roll

Now we're growing in confidence growing so strong
Soon we'll be asking why it took so long
We're not asking for miracles
Looking for fights
We want respect and we want human rights
and we're on the right track now
No turning back now
No one can deny me
This freedom lives inside me

Then I turn on the video
And see all the bright tomorrows
True hearts and new souls
Let the good times roll
Yeah times are changing
Now we have no shame
We are the lovers
Who dare to speak our name

© Nelson/Walsh, IMRO and Peer Music Verlag, 1995

Z r a z y

Lee Fleming

► CLOSING NOTES

Date of birth
October 13, 1957

Place of birth
The largest city in Canada

Astrological sign
Libra, with Capricorn rising:
head in the clouds; hands in
the dirt

Heritage
Hotblooded Irish &
conservative Anglo-Saxon

Languages
English, French, Lesbianese

Current residence
A tiny city on a red, sandy
isle on the east coast of
Canada

Instruments
Vocals, classical & acoustic
guitar, blues harp, percussion

Books
Feminist bookstore co-owner,
1982-87; *By Word of Mouth*,
1988; *Tide Lines*, 1991; *To
Sappho, My Sister*, 1995;
Hot Licks, 1996 (all with
gynergy books)

► ► ►

Music has always been my first passion. I grew up in a musical family and received voice training from an early age from my mother, a talented pianist with a professionally trained voice. Since my early teens, I've been playing music and writing songs. A grounding in reggae and blues came from living in the West Indies in my early twenties; playing street music taught me musical spontaneity; and my current studies in classical guitar and voice have given me the gift of discipline and humility. I am following my dream of recording a CD of original songs. I'll continue to edit books to feed my social, political and intellectual soul. Domestic bliss comes from my partner Heidi and her three great kids. ◄

JACK LECLAIR